Reassembled

"*Reassembled* is an incredible gift of hope and love from Tilden Davis Arnold. Her raw sharing of the many challenges she faced as a young girl will move you to believe that God is intricately at work in our lives, that our humanity is deeply connected, and that beautiful bonds can be forged despite loss. Tilden's story uncovers the blessings of darkness, illuminates the potential for the extraordinary, and will leave you with a profound sense of hope. Reassembled is truly a gift for our times."

—Catherine Goodman Farley, author of *Desert to Dawn, Reflections to Inspire, Refresh, and Renew*

"Loss can reveal what we are made of, and Tilden Davis Arnold's *Reassembled* reveals a beautiful, tender, thoughtful, and wide-eyed girl who you want to get to know more with every page you turn. Within moments of opening this story, I found my eyes glazed over and my heart swollen. Tilden paints a story that reminds us that our most raw, broken moments make us who we are just as much as the most joyous moments. Whether you have intimately experienced loss or not, Tilden's words feel familiar and connect you to the universal experience of vulnerability. Her own intimate story ultimately reminds us of who we are."

—Lucinda Caldwell, founder, Giddy by Nature

"In *Reassembled*, Tilden Davis Arnold writes honestly and openly about rebuilding a young life shattered by loss. In only thirty years of living, Tilden has discovered a clarity and purpose that many people don't find in eighty years of living, if ever. Buy this book for your daughters and then, gift one to yourself. Tilden is wise beyond her years and her old soul has much to say."

—Kathy Izard, author, *The Hundred Story Home and The Last Ordinary Hour*

"Tilden's memoir affirms the paradox and nobility of the human condition: that we only discover ourselves and our purpose when we give up trying to control our world and destiny; that embracing our vulnerability actually strengthens our soul; and that by engaging with those around us, we transform our isolated existence into a community of hope and resolve. Her journey is the sinew of faith."

—Will Speers, former associate head of school, St. Andrew's School

"Tilden Davis Arnold has written a poignant memoir chronicling her life so far. Her narrative takes us on her journey—both inner and outer as her idyllic childhood is abruptly altered by tragic events not of her doing. When divorce, loss, and illness overwhelm, Tilden resorts to control, perfection, and dutiful caretaking of her family that she loves so dearly. It is only when she takes her first steps on her inner journey that self-discovery and healing begin. Tilden's honesty will encourage and inspire all who read the book. I look forward to the sequel."

—Perry Pidgeon Hooks, president, Hooks Books Events

"Tilden masterfully weaves a path of resilience and inner strength through life's unexpected twists and turns. Her survival skills and ability to absorb and learn from each life experience helped her rebuild the puzzle pieces into an authentic life."

—Gib Staunton, founder & principal, Staunton Career Advisors

REASSEMBLED

I hope this reminds you of your
own extraordinary purpose within!

Love always,

Tilden

Unlocking the
Extraordinary Within

Reassembled

A Memoir

TILDEN DAVIS
ARNOLD

Be Bold Publishing
338 S. Sharon Amity Road
#225
Charlotte, NC 28211

tildendavisarnold.com

Book cover design by Dissect Designs
Book interior design by Katy-Whitten Davidson
Editing by Frederica Morgan Davis and Elizabeth Dickens
Author photo by Abigail Wedding Photography

Paperback ISBN 979-8-9861360-0-4
eBook ISBN 979-8-9861360-1-1

This book is dedicated to Warren and Baird,

for walking this journey alongside me,

and for being my life raft.

Without your support, this story would not exist.

And to Alex,

for being my everything.

Contents

PART TWO: DARKNESS

PART THREE: PALACE

Author's Note

I write this book inspired by women before me who have shared daringly. Their stories, like treasured gifts, found their way into my hands and set me free of fear and self-doubt on many occasions.

Encouraged by Marianne Williamson who wrote, "And as we let our own light shine, we unconsciously give other people permission to do the same. As we are liberated from our own fear, our presence automatically liberates others," I hope my words help your own extraordinary light shine a little brighter.

"Imagine yourself as a living house. God comes in to rebuild that house. At first, perhaps, you can understand what He is doing. He is getting the drains right and stopping the leaks in the roof and so on; you knew that those jobs needed doing and so you are not surprised. But presently He starts knocking the house about in a way that hurts abominably and does not seem to make any sense. What on earth is He up to? The explanation is that He is building quite a different house from the one you thought of—throwing out a new wing here, putting in an extra floor there, running up the towers, making courtyards. You thought you were being made into a decent little cottage: but He is building a palace."

— C.S. LEWIS

MERE CHRISTIANITY

Part One

COTTAGE

*"Opportunities to find deeper powers within ourselves come
when life seems most challenging."*
—Joseph Campbell

One

At every wedding's father-daughter dance I cry. I know it's coming, but I still cry. I don't run to the bathroom to try to avoid feeling the pain and sadness that ensues, nor do I try to pretend like I am okay. Instead, I watch in loving admiration as the beautiful bride waltzes across the dance floor, smiling as she lightly rests her head on her father's chest. This tradition is one of my favorites as it reflects the deep love a father has for his daughter. It stands as one last chance for Daddy's little girl to dance in his warm arms, protected. So I watch and I cry because I know that the waltzing little girl in her father's arms will never be me.

◇ ◇ ◇

Three heads popped out from the beige king-size comforter, little bodies snuggled together, waiting for the home video to appear on the television screen. My sisters and I loved pulling out old video cassettes. It was thrilling to watch mini versions of ourselves dance around the screen, transporting us back to a time when the portrayed events had yet to crystallize in our memories.

My dad, wearing thick, round glasses that matched his dark brown hair, reached into the black bag that held about twenty other recorded videos and rummaged around, intentionally stretching out time to build our anticipation. Once he selected a cassette, my sisters and I watched closely as the tape traveled into the VHS converter, and then into the slot at the bottom of the TV.

Within seconds the black-and-white static on the screen was replaced with an image of a beautiful blonde. Dressed in a summer-patterned, oversized mumu, my mom's tan, toned arm flexed as she held a baby carrier a few inches from the ground. The camera followed her as she proudly walked up the narrow walkway to our three-bedroom house in Charleston, West Virginia.

As he held the camcorder steady, my dad's voice gently narrated the scene announcing the arrival of my baby sister, Warren. The blurry date on the right-hand corner of the TV screen read "Aug. 1993." The camera zoomed in on my little sister's face, her eyes closed, deep in her dream world, innocently shielded from all that would come. Then the camera moves to my mom's face as she lightly laughs at Dad's silly filming antics, capturing their pure joy of bringing a second human into the world. This time they would both know what to do, having already had me two years prior. With both my sister and mother in view, my dad whispers, "Welcome home," then the screen goes black.

Three seconds later, I make my special camcorder appearance. My shoulder-length, light brown hair, parted to the side, is held back by a tiny pink barrette. Sitting on my mom's lap, I smile at the camera and share short phrases, eager to understand what is happening but ultimately restricted by my two-year-old language capacity to form full sentences.

My mother's mother, also a petite, tanned figure, enters the screen gently carrying baby Warren in her arms. While thin, my grandmother's arms would hold my sisters and me on many occasions throughout our lives, her embrace bringing the necessary comfort in turbulent times. "Lumlum"—a name she adopted when I tried to say "Grand-mum"—tenderly approaches my mom and me who are seated on the blue couch, and places Warren on my lap. Dad's voice behind the camera chimes in, "Look, Tilden, this is your new baby sister. Can you say hi to your new baby sister?" I cutely respond, "Sister. Baby sister." A questioning tone in my voice suggests I am still trying to figure out what in the world "sister" really means. How this new thing sitting in my lap might change my world. If only I could have more fully understood that this real, live doll baby would become my very best friend, a person who would walk alongside me through thick and thin. This moment was the introduction to the strong bond that would follow.

Caressing her delicate, pale skin with my small index finger, I gently explore the parts of this new baby's face. As my finger glides over her nose, I hear the adults say "nose"; then, sliding my finger from her nose further down her face, I hear them say in unison, "Those are her lips," encouraging this teachable moment of exploration. I continue to trace my finger to one of her ears, then the corner of her eye. I look at Warren's closed eyes and questionably whisper again, "Sister?" and then, more confidently this time, as if realizing she would be mine forever, "Baby sister."

We all tease my mom every time we watch this video because above this intimate moment, my mom's voice peppers concern over the length of my fingernails and with each move of my finger she reminds me that I need to be gentle. Perhaps this is when I began to internalize the societal demand for a gentle demeanor, as being gentle, "lady-like," and quiet would become defining characteristics of my identity as a little girl.

"Look up here," my dad says, and I lift my head, lean back against my mom's chest and together we smile at the camera. We are happy. One big, happy family. My mom, my dad, Lumlum, my new sister Warren, and me.

Then the camera turns off and the TV screen fills with black-and-white static dots, the rest of the tape empty.

Our family of four became a family of five two years later after my youngest sister, Baird, was born. We moved from our little house seen in the video to a three-story, white house with black and white checkerboard flooring in the kitchen and a green rug in the TV room. The large playroom in the basement became a dream world for my sisters and me—a place where we would occupy ourselves for hours with imaginary games of house and restaurant, and games of tag and hide-and-go-seek. The three of us were inseparable—three peas in a pod, as we would say when we got older. My parents, on the other hand, were not as much.

◇ ◇ ◇

My parents, introduced by friends, met in their late twenties. My dad brought home report cards as early as kindergarten that noted his impressive social skills. His second grade teacher to this day shares how Dad was one of her favorite students, describing how he would look up at her, bat his long eyelashes, and, exuding natural charisma, convince her that the class needed a snack. In middle school, he played tennis, his interest in the sport leading him to a position at the US Open as what was then called a ball boy—an achievement he liked to reminisce about at parties. In high school, he traveled up north to attend St. Paul's, a small boarding school in New Hampshire, where he played squash and was treasurer on the student leadership team. After graduating,

Dad attended the University of Virginia where he displayed a wild streak and was reputed to keep parties alive with his creative wit. He was smart and athletic, but most notably, he could light up any room with his loving sense of humor.

My mom tried to tame him like one of the horses she owned in her childhood. Standing 5'8" with soft tan skin, thick blonde hair, and resembling the ultimate tomboy, my mom was naturally beautiful. The heartthrob of many in her early years, she was also a bit rebellious as a teenager, perhaps due to being caught in the middle of divorced parents. She tells stories of traveling to various states, kissing boys, and exploring the world on her own terms, unwilling to be held back by rules. After a stint in Hawaii as a model in her early twenties, she attended American University in Washington, D.C., graduating with a degree in psychology and a minor in special education. She moved to the beat of her own drum, and rather than captivating a room with humor like my dad, she needed no introduction. Mom could walk into a room and simply sparkle; her natural beauty, big heart, and air of rebellion left people wanting more.

After traveling back and forth for over two years between New York City, where Dad lived after college for eleven years, and Washington, D.C., where Mom lived, the two married in October, 1989, after my mom gave my dad an ultimatum. She had had her fun; the wild within her was ready to settle down.

Perhaps never meant to marry, Dad often stayed out late, working at his corporate bank job or attending evening happy hours with coworkers—the social world always a comfortable space for him. As a result, when I was born in July of 1991, my mom experienced loneliness navigating the new world of parenthood alone. She was always there during the times when Dad might not have been. While I don't cognitively remember this chapter in my life, perhaps this early phase of childhood—a stage in which babies rely on their caregivers to develop trust in their world—is where the seed idea of my mother as my hero began to grow.

In elementary school, when teachers asked us to draw our heroes, my classmates might've labored over a red blob meant to be Spiderman, or Disney princesses like Belle or Jasmine, but I always drew a yellow-haired stick figure holding my stick figure hand. My mom was my hero, and her superpowers became even grander the older I grew. There was nothing that my mom couldn't do.

Just as I started to formulate my own memories, around the age of six, we moved from West Virginia—my dad's hometown—to Wilmington, Delaware, where my mom grew up. Though I was unaware of it at the time, my mom's powers were beginning to lose their force, and the move would be her final attempt at holding our family of five together.

Two

While brushing my teeth, I scanned the 'Feeling Faces' paper Mom had taped to the mirror in our lime green bathroom. Warren, Baird, and I shared the bathroom, along with everything else in our two-story ranch house that we moved into when I was almost seven. The house was just five minutes from my mother's childhood home.

The paper taped to the mirror had a smiley face labeled "happy," a face with its tongue sticking out and eyes crossed labeled "silly," and so on. Every morning on the way to elementary school, my mom would ask us to share two or three feelings that we were experiencing. Being a learning specialist, she would not accept a mere "good" an acceptable answer. One morning, this 'Feeling Faces' paper showed up in the bathroom, strategically taped where we could not avoid learning from it during the two minutes we brushed our teeth.

As we got older, and "happy," "tired," and "annoyed" had been used enough times to answer her morning question, Mom required that our answers be even more descriptive. As a result, we found a different page taped to the mirror. This one had no faces—just lists of feelings in alphabetical order. I was amazed to learn that there were over twenty words to describe my internal rumblings. I looked them over, not understanding what many of them meant. But soon I knew that instead of "happy" I could be "joyful," "zippy," "excited," "cheerful," or "exuberant."

After a year of appeasing my mom, by the time I reached third grade I dreaded participating in her beloved game. To make her "happy," I continued to scan the list each morning, selecting three words ahead of time, putting in as little brainpower as I could. I would be ready to go when she asked.

I would pick "calm," "content," and "pleased" on a morning that was moving nicely around our routine, and I might rely on "aggravated," "worried," and "irritated" on mornings when we were running late. To this day I hate being late.

As a student, I also hated being asked to answer a question when I didn't have my hand raised. I rarely raised my hand. More often than not my report cards read, "Tilden is a great student and we love having her in class. We only wish we would hear from her more." My mom, who was never interested in my grades and always interested in the comments, would encourage me to speak up in class, reiterating how important my thoughts and ideas were, but I continually struggled to find confidence in my voice. I was a really good listener, so I preferred accessing my strength.

On the playground, however, I talked all day, organizing games of boys-chase-girls or capture the flag, but there was something about answering questions—all eyes on me—that made me anxious. Or, as the 'Feeling Faces' depicted, a sweaty face with flushed cheeks and a nervous-looking frown. Providing the wrong answer was not an option—to me, it equated to failure. So, to avoid feelings of anxiety brought on by potential failure,

I sat on the carpet or in my desk chair and quietly followed what was asked of me, listening and learning from my classmates and teacher. Never speaking up myself.

Mom's ongoing feelings lesson was put into practice when I encountered my first loss at the age of seven. In addition to the feelings check-in on the way to school, my mom was also all about "family meetings." When a family meeting was called, we were asked to sit in a circle so all eyes could be seen and all voices heard. Anyone could call such a meeting, not just the adults. As if we were her students, during these meetings Mom set group norms that encouraged sharing and inclusivity. Meetings were never about one person telling another what to do and not do, but rather about us as a "family unit," as she put it, having an honest conversation.

"Girls, can you please come upstairs into the living room? Your father and I would like to have a family meeting," Mom called down to us in the basement, using her controlled but serious, voice. My sisters and I exchanged looks, wondering if anyone knew what this might be about. As was expected, we put our toys down and walked up the stairs, knowing that meetings were reserved only for more serious topics of conversation, not the weekend's planned activities.

We entered the living room where Mom and Dad were already seated in separate chairs. The air felt stiff. My mom, evenly-toned, politely asked us to take a seat, so I curled up in the flower-print, wingback armchair. This was my favorite because the arms curved widely, ultimately allowing me to shield my face when I felt like shying away from confrontation. My sisters, who were five and three, and less aware that family meetings often heralded something ominous, shared a seat on the couch, openly exposed to whatever was about to come our way.

Mom began in a delicate but finite matter, "When two people love each other, they often choose to celebrate that love and get married. But when two people aren't in love with each other anymore, they can choose to separate." Then she looked each of us in the eyes, intentionally, perhaps trying to see if we knew what was coming, and explained, "Mommy and Daddy do not love each other like they used to and together we have come to the conclusion that we do not want to be married anymore."

What did that mean?

I was only seven. I loved my mom, my dad, my sisters, and my dog; I couldn't imagine just one day waking up and not loving them anymore.

Our faces undoubtedly looked like we had just eaten handfuls of Sour Patch Kids—trying to determine if this news was sour or sweet. Warren, Baird, and I sat in silence, looking back and forth to one another in an attempt to see if anyone else understood what was just said aloud. Picking up on our facial cues, Mom clarified our confusion by explaining that she and Dad would no longer live in the same house. They were getting a divorce.

Silence swelled as we internalized the news. I tried to wrap my mind around what this word "divorce" would really mean. None of my friends had families that were divorced because both of their parents were in one house when I visited for playdates. *Was divorce a good thing? Could they still love each other without being 'in love' with each other?* I had never heard my parents fight or show any signs that they were not like other parents. *Did they still love my sisters and me?*

Trying to get a better understanding, I broke the silence, "If you guys aren't living together, does this mean we are going to have two Christmases and two Easters?" And my mom calmly responded, "Yes, you could look at it that way."

She explained that my dad had found an apartment less than

five miles from our home. My mom, my sisters, and I would continue living in our three-bedroom ranch house that we'd moved into a few months earlier, and my dad would move out. We would visit him every other weekend and on Monday and Wednesday nights for dinners.

It all didn't sound too bad. Two houses to play in, twice the number of toys, and twice the number of holiday celebrations. It wasn't until a week later when my dad actually moved out and our new routine began that I realized what divorce really meant.

Our family of five was forever broken.

◊ ◊ ◊

My head leaned against the side of the tan felt car interior, eyes locked in focus on the familiar trees lining our everyday, back-road route to school. As our car whizzed along at forty-five miles per hour, the comfort that had once come from the routine drive was blurred—just as the definitive edges of the trees blurred into one, my eyes unable to stop and distinguish just one tree. The landscape mimicked the thoughts and emotions rumbling in my heart and head.

Right on cue, Mom asked, "What are your three feelings, honey?"

Today I did not need to look at the feelings paper to prepare my answer. Taking my eyes off the trees and refocusing them straight ahead on the back of the headrest, my heart spoke for me.

"I am feeling sad, mad, and a little lonely."

I was sad because at the end of each day I would not be able to give my dad a goodnight hug. Mad because I hated that it was my family that was broken and not another kid's. And a little lonely because it had finally hit me that my life didn't look like the families of the other kids in my class. My parents were different. My life was different. I was different.

Though I initially surprised myself by the definitiveness of my response, saying it out loud allowed me to process each emotion for the remainder of the ride.

◇ ◇ ◇

In the months following my parents' divorce, I would delicately tap every eyelash that fell on my cheek with my index finger, draw my finger carrying the lone, black crescent moon to my lips, close my eyes tight, make my wish, and blow it into the universe where, according to folklore, floating eyelashes were supposed to gain the power to make wishes come true.

I wish that my parents would get back together so my dad can come back home and my life can be just like the other kids'.

I wanted so badly for my parents to reunite, not because I wanted them to love each other again, but because I wanted my life to be like my friends'. I wanted my life to be normal. Or at least what I'd deemed as normal at age seven.

While my blown eyelashes never made my wish come true, after a few months I stopped wishing for my parents to get back together. I had to start wishing for something else.

Three

―――

"**O**rder's up!" I yelled as my fingers tapped the top of the silver bell, sending a ringing sound throughout the make-believe restaurant Warren, Baird, and I created in our basement. Three pens dangled from the pocket of Baird's white apron as she talked to the five stuffed bears propped up around a plastic tub turned over to serve as a table.

"Are you ready to order now, Bear family?" she asked kindly, scribbling down their imaginary orders on her small, lined notepad.

As Baird took orders and I cooked invisible food on our children's kitchen set, Warren stood at the makeshift hostess stand greeting more stuffed animal guests. Our restaurant was always busy thanks to Warren. When one person got tired of her assigned role, we switched to give another person a try at chef or hostess. At eight, six, and four years of age, we played for hours downstairs in our imaginary dream world. It was often a perfect distraction to the world our mom lived in right above our heads.

"I have to go to the bathroom," I would say while passing off my chef's apron to Warren. As if the staircase were a portal, with each step I climbed, I shed my youthful imagination and armored up to play the adult. True to my word, I went to the bathroom, but instead of using it to relieve myself, I grabbed a washcloth and soaked it in cold water, wringing it tight so water wouldn't drip on the floor as I walked to my mom's room located on the other end of the house.

Taking a deep breath, I entered the room, trying to peek inside first to see what I was about to walk into. Seeing that Mom was lying on her left side, her eyes closed in a light slumber, I gently tapped on the wooden doorframe, alerting her that I was about to come in.

"Hi Mom, it's me." I whispered, "I came to check on you."

I stepped closer and lightly sat on the side of the bed, noting the beads of sweat from her fever. I softly draped the cool washcloth over her forehead, trying to soothe her pain. On other days if it wasn't a cool compress, it was another temporary fix: a bottle of ginger ale, or a heating pad.

My mom was formally diagnosed with chronic pancreatitis when she was thirty-seven. Chronic pancreatitis is defined as an inflammation of the pancreas that does not heal or improve. It ultimately impairs a person's ability to digest food and make pancreatic hormones. Individuals experiencing this disease often have pain in their upper abdomen or back and the pain can become worse after eating and drinking, which can cause the pancreas to have an "attack."

Born with an abnormally-sized pancreas, Mom's first pancreatic attack—essentially caused by increased stress—occurred at summer camp when she was in her early teens. While she was able to go without another attack for many years, when she was thirty-seven the organ became further inflamed after three pregnancies. Her body was simply unable to undergo more intense stress. As her pain increased, doctors performed a Whipple procedure, ultimately removing parts of the inflamed pancreas. This surgery started what would become years of managing pain, often in the form of strong opioids. Thankfully my sisters and I were too young to remember, let alone fully understand the risks of the procedure.

While hopeful that the procedure would eradicate the issue, Mom's pain worsened and it seemed as though around the time my dad moved out, her disease moved in, ultimately becoming a permanent roommate. To me, her disease was an unseen force that weighed her body down, restricting her to her bed. She sweat or shook with fevers, moaned trying to hold in the sharp pain within her tummy, and slept a lot. Even though I wanted her to wake up and ask about my day, when she was resting, I imagined the disease was often resting too, unable to hurt her.

Checking in on her, I sat by Mom's side for just a little longer, observing in silence, imagining her pain as large, heavy bricks depriving her of freedom. If only the pain was a brick, I often thought, because then I would've been able to try with all my might to pick the bricks up and put them on my own back, taking any bit of her pain away. As her days of pain turned into weeks, and sometimes months, I was endlessly frustrated by my inability to alter her physical condition. I tapped fallen eyelashes onto my index finger, and with each one closed my eyes as tight as I could and asked the universe to free her of pain, to let me be her ultimate protector, her guardian angel. Then I blew the lash away.

"I will always be your angel, Mom," I whispered as she drifted back to sleep. It was a phrase my mom recalls that I randomly started saying to her one day when I was around the age of two. As she remembers, we were driving in silence when I looked up and unexpectedly said, "Mommy, I will be your little angel forever." To this day we both are unsure what instigated me to say it, but it is something I never let her forget.

I tiptoed out of her room, down the hallway, and back down the stairs where I put on my chef's apron and whipped up a new plate of imaginary pancakes. The enjoyment of "cooking" wasn't the same now that I had the image of my mom curled up in a ball in my head, but my sisters deserved to have fun and play. They were allowed to be lost in our imaginary dream world. They were only kids, I would often tell myself, and it was my responsibility to protect that. While I too was a kid, only two years older than Warren, I took on the responsibility of caretaker, believing that if I didn't step up everything would fall apart. In my eyes, our family unit cracked after my parents' divorce, so it was my duty to make sure nothing else happened to cause us to shatter.

Four

Following the divorce, Mom and Dad became like yin and yang. While my parents' houses were only a five-minute drive apart, they felt like two completely separate worlds. It seemed as though their opposite circumstances complemented each other in providing my sisters and me with the balance needed to counteract the illness that lived within the walls of Mom's house. Mom's house was home base—the place I imagined when friends or teachers asked, "How are things at 'home' ?" Dad's house, on the other hand, was equated with adventure. Just like packing for vacation, every other weekend my sisters and I packed our L.L.Bean suitcases and excitedly hopped in Dad's car when he came to pick us up after school. At home I self-enrolled as a caretaker, and, every other weekend when we went to stay with Dad, I exhaled and became an eight-year-old kid.

Whether or not my parents intentionally designed it this way as a result of the divorce agreement, what happened at each house seemed to stay at each house. It was as if there was an invisible bubble surrounding each household containing the separate experiences. In reflection, perhaps I was the one who created this clear division; perhaps it was a defense mechanism for traveling between these two worlds so I wouldn't get my roles—caretaker and kid—mixed up. Either way, my parents seemed to have mutual respect for each other's space. If something went wrong with Mom's health, my sisters and I would call Lumlum, not Dad.

To this day I am not entirely sure how much Dad even knew about Mom's deteriorating health in the early years of their divorce or the extent of my responsibilities as caretaker. In my mind, he didn't need to know because as soon as he came to pick us up on Friday evenings it was my time to shed the hard stuff and have fun. Ultimately, my two worlds became a blessing, an ironic, welcomed twist that was a result of their separation.

While weekends with Mom were unpredictable, never knowing when our imaginary play downstairs would be interrupted by a pancreatic attack, time with Dad was always consistent, both literally and figuratively. Per the divorce the agreement, Dad's designated time with my sisters and me was scheduled for every other weekend and Monday and Wednesday nights for dinner. In the early years of the divorce, the mandate held Dad to a routine schedule; he was required to put work and social obligations to the side in order to report for "Dad duty."

In the ups and downs of Mom's illness, my sisters and I could always count on Dad to not only pick us up, but to concoct a marvelous adventure. On Saturday mornings at Einstein Bros. Bagels, I liked to watch Dad as he scanned the morning paper, its pages already crinkled by a previous reader who left it folded at the edge of the checkout counter. He loved to show us the cartoon page, often sharing a short comic that made him chuckle. Not getting to see him every night made me value our time together, each moment a gift.

My legs swayed back and forth in the air, not quite able to touch the wooden slab connecting the barstool legs together. I shifted my gaze from Dad to Warren and Baird, sitting on the barstools to my left, the two of them busily chatting about something, and smiled. I looked forward to these mornings at Einstein Bros. Bagels, our go-to Saturday morning breakfast spot. Just down the road from Dad's garage apartment, I enjoyed devouring my standard order: a cinnamon sugar bagel toasted with cream cheese and a carton of chocolate milk. Like clockwork, as we ate, Dad would refold the paper and reenter the conversation, asking, "What's on the agenda today?" Bagels were always the appetizer to a "Dad's weekend" bowl of fun. There was an expansive menu of options to choose from. Weather dependent, on some days Warren, Baird, and I opted for an outdoor adventure. Like the time the four of us spent the entire weekend clearing out overgrown brush near his apartment so we could build a fort under the trees. Or when we glamped (glamorously camped) in the backyard in an extra-large tent specifically purchased so we could fit four twin air mattresses inside. The tent came with a front flap that zipped around so we could thread an orange extension cord from the house into the tent to power a small TV, without letting any bugs in. If it was raining, we might choose to visit the movie theater or the mall.

Our favorite indoor activity for a few years was going to Barnes & Noble, but not because we wanted to peruse the books. Instead, my sisters and I would speed-walk past the shelves of books to the listening section at the back of the store, where headphones hung readily available for customers to listen to a featured track on various promoted CDs. There was no doubt that Dad would often *have* to buy a book, his curious mind itching to learn about the next big thing in business, art, and personal development. My sisters and I would giggle to ourselves after recognizing the pattern: Dad would buy a book with every intention of reading it, only to complete the first chapter, and then add it to his "to be read" pile—one of the numerous stacks of books growing in corners of every room in the house. He always seemed too busy to stay with one thing for too long, his innate curiosity ready to explore what was up next.

Dad's creative mind was matched when he met Beth. Beth, a true creative as an artist and a free spirit, gave Dad a run for his money. The first time Warren, Baird, and I were introduced to her—a few months after they started dating and a couple of years after my parents' divorce—Beth told us to take a spaghetti noodle from the boiling pot with a ladle and throw it up to the ceiling to see if it would stick. According to her, the longer the noodle sticks, the more likely it is ready to eat. The next thing we knew, there were about twenty noodles hanging from the ceiling. "Don't worry," she said, "they will all come down at some point." After dinner, we used the leftover pasta to make art. Each noodle was its own unique paint brush as we dumped it into a bowl of paint and flung it up against a large white sheet of paper, a wild squiggle left once the noodle hit the page. Her carefree attitude was exhilarating in comparison to the seriousness I felt I had to portray so often at Mom's house. At Beth's house, there were no rules. It was a sort of lawlessness that I admired but felt intimidated by, feeling like we were always defying a sense of order.

Another time we visited Beth's house she was riled up, excited about another one of her great ideas. I am not sure where Dad disappeared to, but Warren, Baird, and I followed her outside, eager to see what she had in store next. To our confusion, we saw a halved watermelon sitting by itself in the middle of the grass. I wondered if maybe we were going to have a watermelon eating competition. To my dismay, Beth picked up a large machete-looking knife lying on the ground about six feet away from the watermelon and said, "Here, Tilden. You take this and try to throw it into that watermelon." My eyes flew open in shock.

Was she serious? She wants me to hurl this extra-sharp knife into the air and hope that it lands into the watermelon? That does not seem safe.

Perhaps she sensed my hesitation, and turned to my sisters. "Or which one of you wants to try?" Baird, much more daring than I, took hold of the knife and gave it a throw. With a thud, the blade shot into the soft ground. "I want to try!" exclaimed Warren, who was now excited by the opportunity after seeing that perhaps no one could get hurt. Like a game of darts, the three of us took turns throwing this knife at the target with the hope that the blade would hit the center of the watermelon. I will never forget the look on my dad's face when he finally came outside to find us involved in the watermelon massacre. Our mischievous fun came to a quick end.

For Warren, Baird, and me, Beth was an early model of what it looked like to color outside the lines, and she added a lot of joy to our life as she and Dad continued dating.

As we adjusted to the divorce, Dad became more than a source of fun. He was our cheerleader and travel agent. Like other kids my age, I started playing youth soccer for the YMCA when I was eight. Due to Mom's health, she was often unable to take me to games or bring cut oranges when it was our turn (something I never blamed her for because I knew it was out of her control), so even if it wasn't an assigned "Dad's weekend," he started driving my sisters and me to games, and was happy to pick up snacks along the way.

For over five years, Baird, Warren, and Dad sat on sideline after sideline in their blue pop-out tailgate chairs and cheered me on.

"Let's go, T!" I would hear my dad yell, followed by a loud whistle that hit a pitch distinctly his.

There was never any pressure to score a goal, he simply encouraged me to go out there and have a good time.

After Baird started playing soccer in her own age group a few years later, Warren sat with Dad on twice as many sidelines. While Baird and I took home several participation medals and trophies over the years (plastic I proudly held with great regard), one day Dad surprised Warren with a trophy of her own—a multitiered, sparkly gold trophy with a cheerleader on top and a plaque glued to the slab at the bottom which read, "#1 Cheerleader." Dad was someone who celebrated all strengths. As a matter of fact, he found a reason to celebrate anything, especially when there was a reason to go on vacation.

While Mom had dreams of traveling to a dude ranch or visiting Hawaii, her body was unable to handle all the necessary movement associated with getting from Point A to Point B, especially when traveling with three small children by herself. So, it was often Dad who was able to take us on extravagant vacations. With my dad, we learned how to ski and how to catch a wave on a boogie board at the beach. Every year after Christmas we packed up the car and went with him to a luxury hotel in West Virginia where my grandparents—his parents—lived on the property. It was there where I felt like a princess. The doormen, who greeted my grandparents by name, held open giant glass doors granting us access to the most grand place I had ever visited at the time. Holding Dad's hand as I looked around in awe of the enchanting, colorful decor, I felt like I was the luckiest little girl in the world. With Dad, somehow all my worries melted away. Time with him was a breath of fresh air—something I needed to counteract the heightened stress of watching my hero battle a grave disease.

Five

Once a year on our birthdays, my mom relishes recounting her labor experiences. While I cringe at the thought of imagining myself coming out of her birth canal, on my birthday she explains how at two a.m. on the day I was born, a feeling as strong as a lightning bolt struck the top of her belly and zoomed down to her pelvic bone, clearly indicating that the time she had been waiting for was *finally* here. She always emphasizes "finally" as I entered this world two weeks past the original due date; Mom recalls crying to the doctor about having a baby stuck in her belly until Christmas.

Just like a lightning flash, I was out within six hours, my middle and ring fingers held together in my small gummy mouth—something I did well into my early childhood. Mom ends the story by fondly saying, "As soon as you arrived into this world, Tilden, you looked around with your big blue eyes, curiously observing your new environment. To this day you haven't stopped observing the world and I love watching you do so."

Maybe it was hearing this story yearly that led me to value my eyes as the means for observing. When I look in the mirror, deep into my blue-green eyes, sometimes I feel like I can see my soul. For me, my eyes are the window to my intuition, a sort of inner knowing. They allow me to sense if I am about to step into a situation that is out of my comfort zone or when something is not right. They are the portals that allow me to access the world as my own. My big eyes watched my dad move into a two-bedroom garage apartment, and I will never forget the time they watched my mom be taken away from our home in an ambulance.

◇ ◇ ◇

I anxiously peered out the window, my nose pressed hard against the glass, praying I would soon see the large truck with flashing lights speed up our driveway.

How long had it been since I'd picked up the home phone and called Lumlum telling her she needed to come over quickly because something was not right with Mom? Maybe thirty minutes? Thankfully, Lumlum only lived five minutes away and was used to being on call.

How long had it been since she used her phone to call 911? Didn't the medics know that they were supposed to come quickly when there was an emergency?

Five minutes felt like it had been over an hour.

I looked behind me to make sure my sisters had not tried to sneak out of our bedroom where I'd left them with strict instructions to watch the movie I'd popped into the VCR—something I often did when I tried hard to play the role of parent and not of terrified child. They were to stay there until I came back.

Assessing the scene, I checked things off the mental list I'd created over time, given various scares that occurred when Mom's pancreatitis flared up.

Lumlum is with Mom in her room—check.

My sisters are in our bedroom, shielded from seeing our mom in pain—check.

Help is on the way—check.

With all the bases covered, my self-assigned job was to keep watch and use my twelve-year-old Jedi mind to will the ambulance to come. I closed my eyes tight and repeated over and over, "Please come. Please come. Please come."

Every second the white truck didn't appear, my mind wandered to dark places.

Is Mom going to die?

Will I have to raise my sisters?

Where will we live?

Will we move out of this house?

Will we go live with Dad? His new house crammed my sisters and me into one room. I wasn't sure I would be able to live on the top bunk forever.

There were many times my mom would suffer uncontrollable pain when her pancreas became inflamed. More often than not, she was able to handle the pain on her own, tucking herself under the covers, ultimately falling asleep after medicating. But after calling Lumlum at mom's panicked request, I knew this time was different.

Just when I was about to lose hope, feeling consumed by fear of the unknown, I caught sight of a large white object visible through the gaps in the bushy holly trees planted at the edge of the driveway. With a jolt of energy, I quickly tiptoed to my mom's room, trying not to cause a scene that would alert my sisters.

"Lumlum, they're here! The ambulance people are here."

She left the room to meet the EMTs at the door, so I stayed with my mom, who was now lying in a fetal position on the cold brown tiles of her bathroom floor. I watched as she groaned in pain. Her face was scrunched, the soft wrinkles around her eyes sharply defined.

"It's okay, Mom," I whispered, as I tried to gently put my hand in hers. "Help is here." From down the hall I heard the door to our bedroom open, followed by the quick pattering of feet. Stuck between wanting to comfort my mom but feeling like I needed to protect my sisters, I swiftly ran toward the pattering with the hope that I might get to them before they saw the ambulance outside. I was too late.

Baird, about eight years old at the time, was shocked to see the large vehicle followed by two men in uniform dragging a board on wheels out of the back.

"What is going on?" she asked. "Why is an ambulance here? Are they taking Mom away? Tilden, is she going to die?"

I had thought all of the same questions and still didn't know any of the answers. As the oldest, my innate reaction was to continue to protect—a sort of 'Sister Superior' role I created for myself. I felt pressure to model the mom figure that was unavailable to us at that moment as we watched her lie uncomfortably on the hard, flat stretcher that was being wheeled through our living room and out the front door.

If I couldn't heal my mom, I could at least try to protect my sisters' innocence, to be strong in the face of fear. I tried to wrap both Warren and Baird in my small-armed embrace, which turned into more of a sports huddle where I was the coach they looked to for a pep talk.

"Mom is going to be okay. They are here to help." I tried to speak with confidence. "But how cool is it that we get to see an ambulance? Not many people at school get to have their mom put on a stretcher and driven off in an ambulance." I continued to try to make light of the situation.

Once the red flashing lights could no longer be seen from the window where we intently watched, Lumlum calmly returned to the house. In comparison to the chaos felt moments before, everything was eerily still. While she assured us that it would be okay, she didn't provide many more answers.

"We have to 'let go and let God'," I reminded everyone.

It was a saying Mom had taught me at an early age when I was frightened by one of her pancreatic attacks. As we were not a church-going family, 'let go and let God' was really the only time I ever heard her talk about God. When my parents were still together, we attended church a few times, but we stopped going because Warren, Baird, and I were not huge fans of Sunday School, or at least that's how I remember it. For my mom, God was a higher power that did not need to be forced on us. She believed that as young people we should be allowed to build a relationship with God, or a higher power, in our own way, on our own time. So, as a kid, I pictured God as a bearded white man who lived on top of the clouds, sort of like the cartoon character, Zeus, from the Disney animated film *Hercules*. God had large, soft hands that could magically transform any given situation with a snap, just like a magician pulling a rabbit out of a hat. God was the creator of the universe and caretaker of everyone, including the angels who lived up in the clouds. They were always watching over us. God was a busy man, so I tried not to be needy. Asking something of God was only for the most critical matters—like a Genie able to grant only one wish.

But my mom reminded us during challenging times, most revolving around her illness, that there are moments when we are not in control, and in those situations the only thing we can do is relinquish our fears of uncertainty to God. Because of this, I grew up trusting that everything happened for a reason. When things were hard it was because God had a plan.

As a child, while I didn't understand the reason behind my mom's disease, I was confident that it was for a greater purpose. If she was supposed to live, God would make sure she would come home from this hospital visit. But I continued to wish on my eyelashes anyway, hoping each thin lash would find its way to his soft hands as a small, additional message that might change his mind if he ever considered taking her to heaven. I hoped my floating eyelashes would serve as the necessary indication that I was on earth wanting her to be okay.

Sometime after this hospital visit, we were introduced to Esmeralda, Mom's standing infusion pump machine. Naming Esmerelda—"Esie" for short—made "her" feel more a part of our family home and made our rooms feel a little less like a hospital. As I lay tucked into bed, the sound of Esie's wheels rolling against the hardwood floor indicated the closing of a day. The wheels of the IV stand rolled around the house in their normal route, first locking the front door, next the side door, finishing up with turning off all the lights but the one above the kitchen stove, just in case we needed water in the middle of the night. The rumbling of the wheels on the hardwood floor became a sound I associated with safety, like a final tuck in and soft kiss of "goodnight" before dozing off to sleep.

By the time I got to middle school I became intensely aware that other kids didn't have an Esie, or a sick mom. I wanted a plan to keep my sisters safe if there was another unpredictable pancreatic attack or hospital visit. Or, if the unthinkable happened and Mom passed away. To make a plan, I had to fully understand Mom's disease—to grasp the science of what was actually happening.

In eighth grade I chose to research chronic pancreatitis for a science project. Unfortunately, just as we know that googling a health issue makes you think you are dying, my quick investigative research made me instantly more worried that my mom could depart this life at any minute. When I got home that day, I told her we needed to talk and I needed her to be honest. A sort of family meeting, but with just the two of us.

It was a warm evening. I remember wearing short sleeves, my arms free of fabric and warmed by the setting sun. The soft sounds of leaves rustling in the light breeze reminded me to breathe as I took steps to avoid the small green apples that had fallen from the trees lining segments of our driveway, which threaded through an acre of land in the front of our house. As the two of us walked further down the driveway I reached for Mom's hand. Holding on tight, I braced myself for the information I did not want to know but felt I needed to hear. She asked what was on my mind that was so serious and I looked up at her comforting face, the face of my hero, and asked, "Mom, when are you going to die?"

If she was caught off guard by the question, her face didn't show it. Instead, we continued walking, our arms slightly swaying together in unison. She looked down at me, her eyes soft, and true to her honest character, she told her thirteen-year-old daughter the science: her doctors predicted she may only have about five more years to live.

Five more years, I thought.

My eyes began to water, holding back tears with all my might because I wanted to be brave. I am sure she sensed my sudden uneasiness because she stopped me from walking ahead. Gently resting her hands on my shoulders, she looked me in the eyes and said, "But I will not be going anywhere, honey, until you, Warren, and Baird are ready to handle this world without me. And only God knows when that timing is."

I closed my eyes, sealing these words into my heart: *She wasn't going anywhere until I could handle this world without her. And only God would know when that was.*

There were so many times in the years following this conversation when she would be in the hospital and I would think to myself, "Okay, I am ready... I think. Wait, God, maybe I am not ready. Don't let this be the time."

Feeling like I didn't have any control over the day when she might go to heaven, and knowing that I only had five years or less left, I was determined to use my time to build a bulletproof plan.

Six

There are people I know who have back up plans for everything. A rain plan for an outdoor barbeque. A basement full of toilet paper for the inevitable empty shelves after a crazy snowstorm. A box of powdered food in case of an apocalypse.

As an early teen, I had the privilege of never feeling consumed by the fear of environmental unknowns. If it rained on the day of my birthday party, I assumed an adult would know how to pivot to a new plan. If there was a tornado warning, my parents assured us we were safe, appearing unrattled by potential damages it could cause. If there was going to be a snowstorm, I never panicked about the power going out because I felt protected in my home and I trusted my parents to figure it out. These potential challenges felt minuscule compared to the looming possibility that my mom could die at any moment.

After learning she may have only five years to live—a secret I held onto tightly, particularly from my sisters—I would lie in bed at night imagining what life would be like without Mom. Fear often permeated my entire body, like blood pumping through my veins.

Where would we live?

Who would take care of us?

Would I have to change schools?

Who would be there to tell me about love?

To help me on my wedding day?

To teach me how to raise my kids?

Just as my pet hermit crab shed one shell for a larger one, I wondered if I could create a bigger shell so that when the inevitable day came, I would be able to move my sisters and me into it effortlessly, remaining protected and in control at all times.

To build my shell of protection, I concocted secret plans. In the event that Mom passed away, I imagined Dad as the common denominator. He was undoubtedly the constant in the chaos. Perhaps, I thought, Dad could move out of his garage apartment and seamlessly back into Mom's room. But, there was something that didn't feel right about that scenario; ultimately I worried that living in the same house without Mom would be like living with a ghost—too closely surrounded by everything that once was.

As if taking notes on an invisible piece of paper, I crossed out Plan A and began crafting Plan B. With the help of my dad, my sisters and I could sell the house, use the money to buy a new house, and move in together to start over. I hypothesized that the new house would need to be located close to Lumlum so we could continue to support one another. And everything I would do following Mom's death would be in her memory.

In preparation for this plan, I asked Mom to write a bucket list of items she once wanted to do but was never able to because of her illness. I told her I would make it my life mission to get it all done. She was my hero, and in the movies the hero never dies, so

I would live to keep her spirit alive.

Nodding my head in agreement with Plan B, I eased my mind to sleep knowing that I was prepared. I thought, if I could give myself time to really let the possibility of this new life sink in, then maybe things wouldn't be as scary or sad when it actually happened. With a plan, it seemed easier to think *when* Mom dies, rather than being frightened by the *if*. If I could change my mind-set, then I could be in control. There was no more surprising me; I had already been surprised enough. However, while I was con-cocting plans to keep our family afloat, the adults in my life were making plans of their own.

◇ ◇ ◇

One day my mom sat me down and suggested that I consider the option of attending a boarding school. Her request didn't seem too out of the blue since both of my parents went away for high school, but I resisted the idea initially. If I went away, who would manage the chaos? Protect my sisters? Watch over Mom? I had attended the same private school since moving to Delaware in the first grade, so I didn't really want to change for high school or have to make new friends. But, to appease her, I agreed to visit the one boarding school that was only forty-five minutes from my house: St. Andrew's School. If I liked it and could see myself there, I would apply. If I didn't like it or didn't get accepted, I would remain at my present school. With a handshake, my mom agreed to my terms.

A tight knot sat in my stomach on the morning of the campus visit. My armpits were sweating, locked in the stiff J.Crew navy blue blazer specifically purchased for this occasion. It didn't help that Mom was doing what she does best—running late. I tried to hold back my frustration because I appreciated that she was making a huge effort to get dressed and come with me on the tour. After I waited patiently in the car for what felt like thirty minutes, we finally pulled out of the driveway.

In an attempt to ease the internal pressure I felt about my impending interview, I looked to Mom and refocused my thoughts on how this could be the fun mother-daughter day I'd been craving—some special time with just Mom and me. But instead of turning left out of our neighborhood, she did a U-turn and drove back down the paved road we had just traveled.

"I'm sorry, honey. I'm not feeling well. I can't go with you today. It's too much," she said, as she reached for my hand to give it a squeeze, perhaps hoping that I wouldn't be too disappointed. Just as my heart started to swell with excitement, it came crashing down like I had run into a brick wall. As much as it stung, I wasn't surprised. This happened all the time. As soon as I would get my hopes up about doing something special with Mom, plans inevitably changed and I was left disappointed. I was more mad at myself for letting my guard down than I was angry at her.

I often watched other kids with their moms in admiration, ultimately wondering if they knew how lucky they were. If they knew what a special treat it was to help run errands, go to the pool together, or go out to eat, let alone have a meal at the same table together. Over time I began constructing armor to protect myself from the empty feeling that came when my expectations weren't met. I tried not to harp on the disappointment too much because I knew deep down that while my mom was absent, she fought for her life every day, and other moms didn't have to do that. No matter what, she was always my hero. And I would always be her angel.

As we turned into our driveway, I wondered if I needed to call

St. Andrew's to reschedule the interview and tour. Mom assured me I would get there. Even if she couldn't do it herself, she always tried her best to make things happen.

Since Dad was at work, within five minutes Lumlum pulled up in front of the house with a bright smile, ready to pick up any pieces, like she often did. Feeling even more panicked about being late, and rattled by the unexpected change, I straightened my posture, armored up to try again, and opened Lumlum's car door, forcing a smile that masked my frustration and nerves, but above all, my sinking disappointment.

Forty-five minutes later we made a few turns that led us to what felt like the middle of nowhere. As we rolled to a stop, we stared at two imposing pillars—"St. Andrew's" etched in the stone—standing straight ahead.

"You ready?" Lumlum asked, and I nodded my head in awe as we drove through the stone gates and down the paved path, well-manicured athletic fields spreading wide on both sides. Autumn leaves on the trees that lined the driveway danced about in the wind as if they had been told to playfully welcome guests. We pulled through the circle and parked in front of the large wooden doors that stood as the passageway into the closest thing I had ever seen to a castle in real life.

This is a school?

I could go to school here?

People my age live here?

Already running behind, I didn't have much time to "ooh" and "ahh" over the magical land I felt I'd just been dropped into. As quickly as Lumlum hurried me inside, we were greeted by smiling admissions staff and separated. I was whisked off on a campus tour guided by a trendy-looking junior girl, and Lumlum was asked to stay and speak with the admissions counselor. Not thinking we would be separated, I was initially troubled by what the admissions counselor would ask her.

Would Lumlum explain to her that she was my grandmother and not my mother? Would she share that my mom was alive, but often sick, and that's why we were late? I hoped she would include that fact because I didn't want to give the impression that I thought it was okay to be late. What would she ask about me? Would Lumlum mention that I was a good kid and daughter? That I tried my best in my school work? That I was a lady?

I forced my thoughts aside as I exited the large building and walked down a brick sidewalk, my friendly tour guide pointing out the math and science building on our left. I imagined myself coolly walking in and out of buildings on the campus to attend classes and various extracurriculars with my new friends on this beautiful fall day. I imagined it would feel just like how I pictured college, and suddenly I felt like I had aged five years. Perhaps if I attended St. Andrew's I could grow into the person I had been trying to be since my parents divorced. I could be an adult.

When we returned to the admissions office, my grandmother and I traded places. It was my turn to share my story, to make a good impression so that I could be accepted. Still unaware of what Lumlum may have shared, I sat up straight, filling my lungs with confidence, and told the admissions counselor about me—the student, daughter, and sister I was at the time. As soon as I started speaking, the words flowed easily. It felt good to take charge of my story and share it with someone who was interested in learning more about me and what I could bring to her school.

While I didn't realize it at the time, I defined success by what others thought of me. I craved to be accepted for the identity I had worked so hard to create in response to my parents' divorce and my mom's disease to be affirmed. Knowing that attending this school could be a transformational experience, I cared so much about what the admissions counselor thought.

Lumlum and I left thinking that this miniature college had exceeded all our expectations. I saw it as a place to continue to grow into the adult role I assumed at home, and at the same time, Lumlum saw it as a place where I could escape the dysfunction at home and finally be the teenager I was among the happy people.

I applied, and was accepted, giving me the confidence I needed to take the leap to move away in the fall of 2006.

◇ ◇ ◇

The world I lived in before, where I was the caretaker, leader, and protector, was completely altered by the St. Andrew's community. Without my mom nearby I worried constantly that my absence at home would leave everyone in a bad place.

Who will provide Mom with a damp towel for her headaches or fevers? Who will shield Warren and Baird from the looming reality of her death, something they still do not know?

Every phone call I received on my new flip phone sent my nerves into gear as I wondered if it would be the call that would end my newly-started journey of independence.

Ironically my independent journey was my parents' and grandmother's plan for my safety. Lumlum often reminded me how I needed to do what other kids my age were doing. That she could worry about things at Mom's house while I was away. "Go find the person you are without all this chaos at home. Have fun!" But I wasn't sure I knew how. The person I'd known myself to be was one who showed up in times of distress with a hard outer shell. The one that would do anything to save Mom from the body she didn't deserve. The one that needed to be in control in order to know that everything was going to be okay. I wasn't sure I knew how to be just another teenager, how to live my own life with the daily struggles of Mom's illness out of sight.

While distance from home provided me space needed for growth, my departure mandated that my sisters—who were in seventh and fifth grade—assume my role as caretaker for Mom's everyday pains and unexpected emergency situations. It was a role that a part of me wished I could keep for myself so they wouldn't have to take it on, but another part of me was relieved to hand it over—to grow on my own without the thought of pancreatitis at the forefront of my mind. As months passed without seeing my family, I learned to relax in an "out of sight out of mind" kind of way.

Thankfully, living in a dorm with thirty other freshman girls made figuring out what my life could be—without Mom's disease hiding in every corner—pretty easy and very fun.

While I enjoyed hanging out with friends from the minute I woke up to the minute I went to sleep, Warren and Baird were quickly thrown into the front lines at home. It was only when I returned home for holiday breaks that I could *see* how much they had grown in such a short amount of time. Warren stood up straighter, more sure of herself. Baird called the shots, her young heart surrounded by a newfound armor and fearlessness.

Perhaps it was this new shared responsibility of taking care of Mom that changed our relationship, or maybe it would have inevitably evolved as a natural part of sibling growth, but my sisters were no longer tiny hearts I felt I had to protect. They were people with personality, strength, and power of their own. And because of that, our bond grew even tighter as I saw Warren and Baird as not just family, but people I loved as my very best friends.

While I cared about their wellbeing, going away for school provided me with a way out. A fresh start where I could focus on myself. The utopian-like society of St. Andrew's would greatly inform my identity and further develop my foundation. My new home looked a lot like the one I had tried hard to build for myself over the years—a masterpiece of perfection.

Seven

Within the first few months of attending boarding school, it was easy for me to see that St. Andrew's was a special place. My grandmother was in fact right when she commented that everyone seemed happy. Everyone *was* happy. The memories I have from high school are full of joy and adventure. My classmates and I played hide-and-go-seek in the empty art building after school hours, or foursquare on the stone walkway crossing the large back lawn that overlooked Noxontown pond. My teachers expanded my mind in ways that pushed me to think beyond multiple-choice tests and into a world of creative round table discussions about pressing societal issues. Attending a place like this was a privilege, and at fourteen, it was a privilege to be able to escape the constant caretaking responsibility that had become unhealthy at home.

However, without a car or the ability to travel off campus often (though more often than not we never wanted to leave—hanging out on the lawn with our friends was all the adventure we wanted), the community had a way of sucking you into its utopian-like bubble. The grandiose brick buildings where *Dead Poets Society* was filmed served as an incubator for high achieving teenagers. I surrounded myself with friends who were top athletes who would ultimately go on to compete at the collegiate level. Friends who were beyond brilliant and would one day influence our global community. There were singers and songwriters who would go on to become renowned music artists. Artists who could transform a large blank canvases with ease and then beautifully articulate the depth behind their work. There were social butterflies who could draw a room's attention with just one funny lunch announcement. There was even a mastermind beatboxer who could sing and beatbox *Somewhere Over the Rainbow* at the same time.

By my sophomore year my head was on a constant swivel, always comparing myself to the high achievers around me. I played three sports, but wasn't the best at any of them. I earned A's and B's in my classes, but wasn't the top of my class. I had a great group of friends, but I wasn't class president. The more I saw those around me excelling, the more I felt like I was fading into the background.

As if to counteract my feelings of inadequacy, perfectionism grew in me like a weed, wrapping itself tightly around any innocence that remained. I fed myself on what I believed to be the truth: the harder I worked to become perfect, the closer to perfection I would become, ultimately invincible to disappointment, failure, and shame.

Perfectionism became my armor needed to battle my feelings of self-doubt as it fueled my competitive edge. Maintaining a positive outlook, I would try to remind myself if I wasn't the best now, that didn't mean that I couldn't be the best one day. So I pushed myself in my school work, accepting nothing lower than a B. Pushed myself in athletics. Pushed myself in my art. I sought to deepen my relationships with friends and faculty. I was elected president of my class junior year and delved deeper into my commitment to community service by leading our school's blood drive.

Like a ticking time bomb waiting to explode, my perfectionism kept winding me up, pushing me further and further to do my best. No, to *be* the best. No mistakes allowed, just success. And success was often defined by others' approval of me, such as being elected captain of my field hockey team, getting an A on a paper, or having an admissions staff member ask me to be on a student panel. For a while I'd found my rhythm. My level of stress was manageable because the reward of feeling confident in my ability to do it all fueled me.

However, over time my body became exhausted by the pressure. At boarding school, I didn't have my parents to wrap me in a loving embrace and tell me to slow down. They weren't there to tell me it would be alright, that I didn't have to keep stretching the boundaries my body tried to remind me I had. I learned an incredible sense of independence and self-reliance, but the reassurance I needed to remind myself of my own humanity was absent. There was no one to tell me that I was never meant to be a robot. And so, I continued chugging along, striving to meet the high expectations I set for myself.

One fall afternoon, I laced up my cleats before running out on the field hockey field to warm up and felt a tightening in my chest. Shaking it off, I joined my teammates in line to make a lap around the field. As we ran, the pressure continued to build, like a tiny person inside me knocking hard to get out. I demanded it to stop, internally telling my mind to focus on the game.

We continued to warm up. My insides felt empty and at the same time so full, tears built up behind my eyes, waiting to be released.

What was happening?

There was no reason for me to cry. My mom wasn't in the hospital. The rest of my family and friends were safe. I blinked several times, popped my mouth guard in and jogged across the field to my position on the forward line. Within five minutes of the starting whistle, I couldn't breathe. My chest was tighter than ever and the more I told myself to 'suck it up and play the game', the harder it was to hold back the constant beating inside. I ran to the sideline asking for a quick sub. My coach asked if everything was okay, as it was odd for me to voluntarily leave the field.

"I'm fine," I muttered, trying with all my might to contain myself. "Just needed a quick sip of water. I'm ready now," I said, hoping that if I could convince her, maybe I could convince myself. The game went on and I played abysmally. I was completely deflated.

Glancing up at the scoreboard, I continued to wish that time would move faster so I could relieve myself of my cleats and uniform.

"Go, T!" I suddenly heard ringing from the sidelines of cheering parents.

It couldn't be, I thought. My dad had visited for Parents' Weekend, but never for a random Saturday game because he was often busy with my sisters at home.

"Let's go, T!" I heard again, and stopped in my tracks to scan the sideline.

Perhaps he could see how much I was struggling, that my gas tank had finally reached empty, because there he was, dressed in his oversized khaki shorts and blue polo, clapping his hands and cheering me on. My dad had come to see me play; he was there when I needed him the most and he didn't even know.

Just like that, the floodgates opened and tears spilled from my eyes. I ran to the sidelines and told the coach to put in a sub. For the last five minutes of the game I cried in my dad's arms. In his embrace I felt weightless, the stress of my world melting off my shoulders. His warm arms replaced my daily armor to be strong, to be perfect. I was transported back in time to before my parents' divorce, the time when things felt easy in my imaginative world of play, when I first started exploring the world within the safety of my parents' love and guidance.

In Dad's arms I poured out my feelings of exhaustion and inadequacy. He looked me in the eyes and told me exactly what I needed to hear: "I am proud of you, T, just the way that you are."

Letting his words sink in, I snuggled my face deeper into his chest. I took a deep breath, inhaling his familiar, calming smell. It was as if Dad's embrace was the secret code needed to deactivate the time bomb of perfection ticking deep within.

After the game was over, he told me to grab my swimsuit. Suit in hand, we drove ten minutes down the road and parked in front of a hot tub retail store. The next thing I knew, our father-daughter catch-up time was accompanied by the luxury of spa jets after telling the clerk we were there to "try out" hot tubs. In typical Dad fashion, he had somehow creatively constructed just what I needed—a time to release stress, to relax, and to just have fun.

I wished we could've stayed in that hot tub forever, free of stress and self-inflicted pressures. Wished I could've seen myself the way he did—proud of my accomplishments. If I did, perhaps I might have learned from this moment that perfectionism is a never-ending tunnel to a goal impossible to reach, but I didn't. Instead, I continued to walk in circles where I set high standards for myself, only to become exhausted and overwhelmed trying to meet them.

By the twelfth grade, the time when applying to colleges exacerbates comparison, I was ashamed and frustrated for being what I considered "average."

Eight

Per Dad's chauffeur role, there was no question about who would take me to tour various colleges when the time came. By her sophomore year, Warren moved away to attend a boarding school of her own in New England, leaving Baird the only one at home. With one less daughter to drive around for school, sports games, and other extracurriculars, Dad had some more time to dedicate to planning our college touring adventures.

I didn't exactly know what I wanted to major in, I wasn't a highly recruited Division I athlete, and I hadn't even narrowed down my ideal college size or location. So, with open minds we started looking at liberal arts schools near my home. We visited Franklin & Marshall and Gettysburg; then thinking maybe I wanted to play Division III field hockey, we moved our search north, visiting Tufts, Wesleyan, and Trinity. While we were in the area, we added Boston University and Boston College to the list. Then it snowed. And it really snowed. I questioned if the frigid winters were really for me. As a result, our college-seeking adventures pivoted: we began to look at schools in the south.

After the eighth college campus visit, Dad and I were like Bonnie and Clyde, finding our rhythm in scheduling tours or walking/driving a campus by ourselves. I was tasked with keeping notes in my journal and assigning each school a number (1, 2, or 3), based on my initial impressions. In my dad's terms, a '1' was assigned to any college that was "the pits," whereas '3' meant "my life will be transformed if I have the chance to attend this college." A decimal system was allowed, given that I had only three numbers to choose from, so my 4x6 spiral-bound notebook became filled with pages that had the name of a college written at the top followed by a number most likely between 2.3-2.6. There weren't any universities that had yet earned a flat-out, life-changing '3', nor a bottom-of-the-pits '1'. Although, one college visit came close to a '1': not because the college itself was bad, but because Dad fulfilled his role as "embarrassing father."

At this particular college, Dad and I found ourselves in the back of the group as we listened to the student tour guide point out various buildings as we passed by. I liked staying toward the back of the group—Dad and I could whisper valuable or silly comments to each other without having to interrupt the flow of the tour. As the guide continued to slowly walk backwards, he asked if anyone had any questions. Visitors looked around at each other in silence, gauging if someone wished to speak up. After a few seconds my dad cleared his throat and I cringed in anticipation of what he might say as he was known to fill any silence with a little laughter and would never turn down an opportunity to embarrass his daughter. "Yes I have a question," he began. "Can you please tell me a little bit about the boys here?" Then: "How are the parties?" The socialite within him needed to confirm that there was more to the college than learning. "Don't feel like you have to answer that," I quickly interjected. My cheeks turned bright red and I elbowed him in the side, ultimately making a note to never return to that campus due to total humiliation.

After visiting almost twenty places, we were experts in college touring (and going a little crazy). Much to Dad's excitement as an alum, the University of Virginia was featured on the map of our southern college tour. Per the usual shenanigans, we ditched the guided tour this time in order for him to give me a personal tour, and then we made it in time for the always dreaded (but helpful) information session. The session was held in the Rotunda—a grand setting that made even the temporary rows of stackable chairs feel formal. In comparison to the inside of Dad's old fraternity house we had just visited—a place I imagined him as a college boy goofing off with friends—I suddenly felt uneasy, intimidated.

Because Univeristy of Virginia was his alma mater, when the information session came to a close and prospective students and families began to clear the room, I was coerced into introducing myself to the man who led the session, as my dad always championed the idea that a personal interaction left a stronger impression than a paper transcript or application. To my surprise, the tall man said he had a few extra minutes to talk. We followed him to his office where he invited me in, and asked my dad to wait in the common area. As soon as the door closed I realized I was locked into an impromptu interview I wasn't sure I was ready for.

I had no time to prepare, let alone time to conceptualize what was happening before I found myself sitting in a brown leather chair across from the admissions officer, trying to discreetly dry my sweaty hands on my pants. The man asked my name, how the college visit was going so far, and then jumped right into his first question.

"Can you tell me about the hardest thing you have done in your life?"

Are you kidding me? I anxiously scrolled through memories as if I was scrolling through channels on TV. I knew what I was looking for—something to do with my mom's pancreatitis—because pancreatitis had been the center of everything hard that had happened to me since my eighth birthday. While there were many hard moments that stood out, I remembered a conversation that was in a league of its own.

My mom was in and out of the hospital so many times during my childhood that a call from my grandmother saying she was in the hospital began to feel normal after I went away for high school. 'Normal' didn't mean that with each call my heart wouldn't sink for just a second in brief panic, wondering if this was the time she might leave this earth, but I'd become immune to it. Becoming immune was the only way I could move on with my day.

However, one night during my sophomore year of high school I lay with the lights out, curled under the covers, cell phone touching my ear listening to my mom's soft voice on the other end of the call, from the hospital. Inside the dark cave of my comforter I noticed for the first time that Mom's suffering wasn't only in her voice, it was also coming from deep within my own heart. It was as if her pain had traveled with her voice from cell tower to cell tower and into my body. I could tell she was working hard to have a normal mother-daughter conversation, but as I listened to her voice, all I could do was imagine myself in her shoes. I imagined the inherent loneliness that comes from lying alone in a sterile hospital bed. The fear derived from a disease she never asked for nor deserved. The overwhelming pain constraining her ability to laugh and be free.

As I hung up the phone, I felt a tear slide from my eye onto my pillow. I had often begged her not to leave my sisters and me on this earth without a mom. On numerous occasions, I had even asked her to be the strong person she was and to fight through the pain.

But what about her? What did she want? I had never considered this until I vividly imagined what her daily experiences were like; she was trapped inside a body that didn't allow her to live fully. After that phone call I knew the next time I saw her I wanted to say something different.

A few weeks later, my mom pushed through her overwhelming daily nausea in order to pick me up from boarding school for fall break. On the forty-five minute drive back to our home we spent the first fifteen minutes or so sharing normal small talk, excited to see each other for the first time in a few weeks, and then conversation dwindled and silence filled the space.

My heart was racing. I knew what I wanted, *needed*, to say to her. But I was scared. I wasn't ready to put the words out into the universe. Once I said them, I could never take them back.

I collected my thoughts, looked over at my mom—this beautiful person trapped in a body wracked with pain—inhaled my courage and said:

"Mom, I know you promised that you weren't going to leave us until Warren, Baird, and I were ready to live on this earth without you. And I appreciate you staying here for us. But I want to let you know that it's okay to die. I give you permission."

I give you permission to fly high and be in a better place. I give you permission to be free. I give you permission to let go—for your beautiful soul to run wild.

I tried so hard to be brave, to mean the words I said. But the weight of saying the words out loud, of saying good-bye to the person who, more than anyone in the world, I did not want to tell good-bye, was overwhelming. As my eyes filled to the brim, her eyes twinkled with tears that seemed not of sadness but rather of relief. She gently replied, "Thank you, T. That is one of the nicest things anyone has ever said to me." *Thank you.*

I blinked a few times, swallowing back the tears that had started to form and clasped my hands together trying to bring my mind back to the present moment. I looked at the tall, stern man who sat across from me in his office, and I said, "Letting my mom go is the hardest thing I have had to do in my life."

It felt uncomfortable sharing something so intimate with a complete stranger. I wondered if I had said the wrong thing or said too much. Perhaps he was simply expecting me to say how sometimes I am too organized or that I am a person who strives for perfection—something typical of a college applicant.

While I can't remember his reaction, I vividly remember the epiphany that hit me hard as I recounted my experience. It seemed as though until the moment when I looked my mom in the eye and granted her permission to let go—to end the fight for my accord—I had been playing a game of tug-of-war with God. With each hospital visit I would pull harder, using my strength here on earth to keep her present with me, ultimately fighting to win the eternal war, for my mom to keep living. On the other end of her suffering—the opposing force of the rope—I envisioned God up in the clouds in heaven. For most of my childhood I felt like I was constantly battling God's pulls—each hospital visit was a time when the middle ribbon dividing the tug-of-war rope was closer to God's side in heaven, an indication of potential divine triumph. But when I told Mom that she could let go, I realized that I also let go. Not because I was tired of fighting for her to remain on this earth—I knew I had a fire in me that would never give up on her—but because I realized after our phone call the reason I was fighting for her existence on this earth was for *me*. I was fighting so that I could have a mom.

As the admissions officer politely escorted me out of his office,

I reconnected with Dad who had been waiting outside. He was completely unaware of the stiff environment I'd been forced into and the story I had shared. I wondered what his reaction would be to me sharing this with someone we had never met before. Would he think I had overshared, and be embarrassed by my lack of discretion? Or would he look at me in awe as I hoped the admissions officer did? I had faith in the latter, but after spilling my heart under pressure just a few moments before, I wasn't up for retelling the story again. I simply told Dad what happened behind the closed door was interesting and certainly more challenging than I was prepared for. If classes were anywhere close to the experience I'd just had in the admissions office, I was not sure the University would be the right fit for my more timid nature. If Dad was disappointed that the place where he had so many fond memories would not be mine, he did not show it. Instead, he smiled and said, "Well how about we go and get some ice cream then?" We got to the car and I scribbled down my impressions of the visit in the small notebook, marking a '2' at the top of the page.

As we drove away I smiled, relaxing my head against the headrest as I watched the clouds go by. I thought about how Mom was close to surpassing the projected five-year statistical likelihood of survival. Reflecting on my new epiphany, I wondered if this memory I'd recounted in the office had become not just the hardest thing I'd ever done, but perhaps it was the single most powerful. In letting go of the rope I'd imagined keeping Mom tethered to earth, I didn't feel God pulling back. Instead, I was rewarded with a miracle I didn't think was possible: extended time with my mom.

Nine

"You're going where?" my friends from home would ask. Of the twenty colleges Dad and I visited, I unintentionally chose to attend the only one we didn't tour together: Sewanee: The University of the South. While the numerous tours were exhausting, seeing a diverse group of campuses allowed me to better understand the necessary characteristics that would ensure a good fit for me. I was seeking a college that would nurture my love for learning, give me the opportunity to play field hockey in some sort of capacity (Division III, Club, or Intermural), and—as I am my father's daughter—would also be a place that allowed me to let loose and have some fun. After a weekend on-campus visit with a friend, it was obvious that Sewanee met my requirements and more! My friends from home, most unaware of the small liberal arts school, couldn't quite wrap their heads around why I would choose to attend a college that was in the middle of nowhere. But, as soon as you arrive on the campus—often referred to as the Domain—it's easy to understand Sewanee's appeal.

For those, like my peers at the time, who don't know about this little slice of heaven located on top of a mountain at the southern end of the Cumberland Plateau, Sewanee is a place like no other. Similar to St. Andrew's, it's more than just a campus. As the legend goes, when Sewanee was created it was so beautiful that angels opted to live in it themselves. Today, everyone who sets foot on campus is given a Sewanee angel for protection. When you drive through the entrance gates you tap the roof of your car releasing your angel, and when you pass back through the gates to leave, you tap again, "grabbing" your angel for protection while traveling off the Domain. While it may sound odd, this tradition is one of many that made Sewanee an incredible choice for furthering my personal development. Like a secret password, tapping the roof each time enhanced my sense of belonging. In my experience, it was a place of refuge, a place where students and professors knew me by name.

A few weeks after Dad helped me unpack into my dorm room, it became evident that Sewanee was a larger version of my high school; the majority of students lived on campus, ate together at the dining hall, engaged in sports, and no one wanted to leave. The campus also looked like Hogwarts, and people actually wore black robes—another unique Sewanee tradition where students are given a black gown to wear as a symbol of academic achievement.

After catching up with friends from high school, my quick comparison solidified just how unique my experience was, especially when it came to my social life. I had friends at larger colleges who couldn't attend parties unless they were on some sort of list, unlike at Sewanee where students moved freely in and out of fraternity house weekend parties. Seventy percent of the student body engaged in Greek life. Unlike traditional sororities, the majority of Sewanee's were local and did not adhere to traditional bylaws, which, in my opinion, created a foundation for authentic friendships and community.

After my freshman year, I proudly reported in my journal that I'd made it through the year with high marks in academics, got playing time on the field hockey field, was initiated into one of the local sororities, made some incredible friends, and was introduced to a senior boy who would become my boyfriend for the next year and a half. It felt like all the pieces of my identity that started forming in my adolescence were naturally sliding into place. At nineteen, I was convinced I had found my stride, and, as I wrote in my journal, "Life is amazing!"

I continued to journal about my personal growth, acutely aware of how I was thriving within the perimeter of Sewanee's safe environment. Eager to share, I would excitedly text Dad to let him know I scored a goal (I played on Sewanee's DIII field hockey team) or call Mom when I found out I was going to be inducted into the Order of the Gown (Sewanee's society of academic distinction) at the beginning of my sophomore year. I enjoyed checking in with my sisters to see how their time in boarding school was going; Baird had recently joined Warren at her school in New England, where they were now a sophomore and senior.

My relationship with my sisters continued to strengthen as I actively worked hard to let go of the feeling that I had to be their protector. In my absence at home over the years, Warren and Baird had proven how strong they were on their own, lovingly supporting Mom during the unexpected pancreatic attacks she continued to experience. As if I was a mother watching her children grow up, I watched them grow into beautiful, brave adolescents. Being away at school afforded them the same opportunity I was given, and I was comforted in knowing that it was now their turn to shed the weight of caretaker duty. It was time for them to spread their wings and more fully become agents of their own life stories, which they did with ease. Warren was elected president of the school her senior year and Baird was given an award recognizing her leadership, sportsmanship, and athletic ability her sophomore year. Watching them thrive in a similar safe environment filled me up even more. There was nothing in this world that meant more to me than my sisters. Amidst the inevitable decline in Mom's health, it seemed as though over time Mom, Warren, Baird, and I had all become warriors in our own ways, adapting to her disease and any curve balls that were thrown at us.

For the first time in a long time, I finally felt like I had things under control. Life was the way I wanted it to be.

Ten

I cracked open the spine of my new black leather-bound journal, a Christmas gift from my mom. At the top of the page I scribbled the date: "December 31, 2011."

The day before my birthday, in July, and the last day of the year have always been big journaling days for me. I intentionally set aside time to reflect on my annual accomplishments and set goals for the upcoming one. Twenty eleven had been an incredible year, but 2012 promised to be even better. I was in the middle of my sophomore year and had plans to travel abroad in the summer, Warren was going to graduate from high school and choose where she would attend college (ultimately choosing to join me at Sewanee!), and Baird was accomplishing great things during her sophomore year in high school, so I made it my New Year's resolution to not just write reflections a few times that year, but to write at least a sentence in my new journal every single day.

To christen my very first day of writing and to wrap up the last day of 2011, as tradition, I made a list of goals I wanted to accomplish in 2012. In my tiny handwriting I listed:

-Academically, continue to follow my love of learning and get all As and Bs.

-Athletically, continue to eat healthy, stay active, and advance as a player on the field hockey field.

-Personally, continue to be inspired and to inspire others.

-Given the opportunity, travel to Spain in the summer.

-Extracurricularly, apply to be a Canale intern (a service internship provided by the college). And apply to be an Arcadian (an admissions tour guide).

-Socially, make more time for my friends and visit those who live in other dorms.

-Strengthen my thoughts and beliefs, and take time to reflect on my identity.

-Be thankful for each day, which I can accomplish through new daily reflections.

-Lastly, continue to build a healthy relationship with my boyfriend, who fills me with love.

I seemed to have missed, "don't forget to give yourself grace," but grace was never part of my achievement plan. I felt free to be my own person, the core of my identity no longer defined by my response to my mom's disease. With a newfound confidence—affirmed by my accomplishments—perfectionism and control were becoming traits I relied on for continued happiness. I chose to set high goals in each area of my life in order to continue to achieve my idea of success—to be the best student, athlete, friend, sister, mentor, and community member that I could be. By the middle of 2012, the end of my sophomore year, I was able to accomplish almost all of my goals. Each of these accomplishments acted as another check mark on the to-do list I lived by, ultimately boosting my self-worth.

Feeling good about the end of my sophomore year and what I'd achieved, to kick off the first week of summer I jumped on a plane to visit my boyfriend, who, at the time, I was convinced was the love of my life. We had successfully accomplished dating long distance for an entire year, something I was not sure I was going to be able to commit to, but in my eyes he was worth it. My Type A personality was dedicated to doing whatever was necessary to be the best girlfriend and making it work.

This early summer trip, however, was different. Things that had seamlessly meshed without much effort felt forced. It was as if we were trying to dance a waltz we'd previously mastered but were now stepping on each other's toes, our body language awkward. Blaming the initial discomfort on the amount of time that had passed since we had last seen each other, I tried to reassure myself that our love for each other would outlast any bumps in the road. But with each day the awkwardness persisted. It was evident that in the last year we had both grown as individuals. I was focused on accomplishing my list of goals and thriving in an environment that supported my growth; he was trying to find his place in the post-graduate world. For the first time, our age gap proved to get the best of us.

Before he dropped me off at the airport at the end of my trip, we went for a long walk and finally confronted the elephant in the room; we were (healthily) growing as individual people, and, just like flowers in a pot, in order to continue to grow, we needed more space.

We were breaking up.

Talking about it out loud during our walk made sense. We were acting as adults who respected and loved each other too much to try to hold on to a relationship that, as evidenced by this visit, had lost its spark.

In our final embrace, the word "good-bye" got stuck in my throat. He whispered good-bye, and I walked toward airport security trying to ignore the sudden rush of emotions. A moment of weakness broke my strength and I looked back one last time.

Was I really ready for this to be over? Was this the right decision?

Looking for a sign that might solve my internal doubt, I searched for him in the crowd of strangers, but he was nowhere to be found. I had officially failed my goal of continuing our relationship.

I chose a seat at the gate facing a large window so that I could hide my tears from the strangers waiting to board the flight. I reached into my pocket to text someone, in need of a quick distraction so the floodgates that held back tears wouldn't be released. Out of habit, I began to type in his name and then quickly realized I could no longer text him. I could no longer call him. The person that I'd shared the everyday bits of my life with for the last year and a half was no longer available. No more good morning texts, no more daily check-ins, no more funny jokes to brighten my day. I stared at my phone hoping it would vibrate in my hands. That someone would text me about anything, demonstrating that there was someone else in my circle who could fill this empty void.

Nothing.

Silence.

This unforeseen change stung. Since arriving at Sewanee I felt in control of my life—my movements, my accomplishments, my attitude—but the weight of this one failure instantly crushed previous worthiness that stemmed from multiple accomplishments. Realizing that intensely staring at my phone would not magically make a text message appear, I typed a message to my sisters. Trying to mask my feeling of loneliness, I typed ever so coyly,

"Guess who's single?!"

Once I got back to Delaware, I stayed in my room, my pillow wet from tears. I walked around the house sulking, feeling empty without the exchange of conversations that once were. After a few days, however, I tried to adjust my mindset, in an attempt to confront and overcome my feelings of failure.

I don't need a boyfriend to be my best self, I reassuringly tried to convince myself, *I am strong just as I am.* My personal pep talk worked on some days, but on others I simply felt lonely at home. My sisters weren't back yet for summer break, my best friend was in Africa, Dad nights were only twice a week, and my mom was, as usual, consumed by her illness. All I wanted was for her to be able to sit at the dinner table with me so that I wouldn't have to sit in silence with my thoughts. But what I had was a mom caged in her bedroom, sleeping on and off throughout the day, drowsy from constant medication.

One night, utterly defeated, I stared at a lonely bowl of salad and my mind began to wander. In a little over a month I would turn twenty-one, so, I thought, *I could sit here staring at lettuce leaves or I could change my attitude and go find myself.*

It seemed up to this point my identity had become checkboxes, and my soul followed the directions it was given to get from Point A to Point B in order to check the box. All I knew was how to mold myself into the container created by my lived environment, heavily influenced by societal rules and norms. But, sitting at the kitchen table as a newly-single young woman, a box in my life plan had become unchecked and I wasn't sure I knew what to do next.

Eleven

In my thirty years of experience I have found that when you are meant to do something, or meant to meet a specific person, these experiences and people often show up in our lives at just the right time, like a puzzle piece that longs to find its designated home in order to help complete the puzzle. Sewanee's Summer in Spain study abroad program was one of those experiences. It was a six-week program led by Sewanee professors providing the opportunity to travel abroad without missing field hockey in the fall. As if on purpose, my trip to Spain would bring a natural new beginning. A fresh start that would not only allow me to move on, but would introduce me to the incredible beauty that comes with a detour in an intended life plan. Similar to my experience applying to high school, I was excited by what the program offered, so I didn't look into other options—I was set on Spain.

After applying, I found out that the program included a three-week, 250 mile walk on the famous pilgrimage, Camino de Santiago. I love walking, so the idea further piqued my interest.

However, as I learned more about the history of the Camino, more specifically the sacredness of the pilgrimage, I was worried my walking might feel fraudulent.

A pilgrimage is typically defined as a journey where a person goes in search of a new meaning about self, others, nature, or a higher good. As a friend simply explained, "People often go on pilgrimages in search of a spiritual awakening." I had initially chosen this trip because it checked the boxes of fun travel, good people, and academic credit which would put me ahead. While I wanted to spend this year reflecting on my identity, I hadn't really considered confronting my spiritual identity; my faith was something that I more often than not ignored in my adolescence. Up to this point in my life, my relationship with God was mainly unexplored. I grew up trusting that things happened for a reason, and God was watching over me from above. I believed God was there when I needed him, and helped others when I didn't. Our relationship just scraped the surface as everyday distractions kept me from really diving deeper into my spiritual beliefs.

Newly single and almost twenty-one, I was eager to soak in the Spanish culture and bars. I itched for the thrill of great adventure, imagining myself rendezvousing through Madrid on the back of a handsome Spaniard's motorcycle like the Olsen twins did in the late 1990s movie, *Passport to Paris*.

I spent two weeks in Madrid exploring museums, bars, and trying my best to speak Spanish (and, unfortunately, not riding on the back of a hot Spaniard's motorcycle), but when it came time to settle my feet into my walking shoes for the first time, I woke up feeling a little nervous.

Just like standing at the starting line of a race and taking a moment to appreciate your body for what it is about to do, I stood at the trailhead of the Camino de Santiago (known as 'the Way of St. James' in English) in Roncesvalles trying to collect my thoughts before taking the first step. Having never walked a path with such historical and religious significance, it seemed appropriate to honor the millions of pilgrims who walked before me following the Way of St. James. However, it was hard to quiet my mind for a moment of silence when I was consumed with logistical concerns. *How would I know where to go? Would I be able to easily identify where our group was supposed to stop for the day?* Once I stepped over the line my journey would begin, but unlike my two weeks in Madrid, it would be without a map. Pilgrims were simply instructed to follow yellow scalloped shells and arrows imprinted on stone milestones that we would see along the route, and to trust in the way.

With my first step forward, I cautiously embraced the unknown road ahead. I was keeping an eye out for the first yellow scalloped shell so I wouldn't make a wrong turn. Just the thought of veering off course sent me down a dark rabbit hole of fear: *What if I get lost? Do I even know how to say "lost" in Spanish? What if I end up walking miles past a turn and don't have enough energy to turn around and walk back to the correct path?* Even worse: *What if I end up like the girl in the Liam Neeson movie,* Taken?

Thankfully, my Sewanee crew and I walked together as a group for the first few miles, allowing my tightly wound anxiety to relax a bit. I enjoyed passing chickens, cows, and other pilgrims on the way—an initial indicator of just how unique this walk would be in comparison to the hikes I did back at Sewanee with friends. Once I found confidence in my stride, I broke from the group with two other girls as our natural walking pace was quicker than the others. All my fears became a reality when in fact we did get lost, but a kind man who spoke a little English turned us back in the right direction (*and* we weren't taken!). Funny how sometimes fear can consume an entire experience until the feared moment actually happens and it's not so scary after all.

Relieved, my mind relaxed, and I felt able to more fully commit to the adventure of the unknown with a "can't turn back now" attitude.

As my body released tension, appreciating the once-in-a-life-time feel of the physical journey, my internal journey began to transform. With each step I was able to be more present with my surroundings—in awe of the earth's natural beauty. The views on the Camino the first day were unlike anything I had seen. There was a stretch of road where I felt like I was on the set for *The Sound of Music*, the rolling hills and mountains silently mirroring my heart's tune. Other parts of the road weaved under pine trees like the forests I'd hiked back home; the soft brown needles created a cushion for my feet. My favorite part of the day was when the trail cut through an expansive meadow of wildflowers, each colorful flower like a unique dot on a pointillism painting.

After fourteen miles, we stopped to treat our exhausted feet to a cool-down in a creek while we waited for the others. Day one was a success. Our feet had escaped without any blisters, morale was high, and conversation was light.

Other than my black Keen sandals that I fashionably wore with socks to avoid blisters, each day I looked like I was about to run a race; I suited up in my favorite black athletic shorts and a quick-dry T-shirt purchased specifically for this adventure. My hair was tied up in a ponytail, and in my black backpack I carried other essentials I might need during a day of hiking: water, sunscreen, my journal, a hat, a light pullover, and a rain jacket. Unlike other pilgrims on the road, my pack was significantly smaller and less full. Others carried their belongings for the entire experience on their backs, whereas a bus drove our group's suitcases to our next destination. My feelings of being a fraud heightened walking without my heavy baggage; it felt like cheating, but there was no denying that I didn't appreciate the luxury. Over the first few days my pilgrimage experience felt just like my faith—a bit superficial.

Continuing to be surrounded by incredible changing landscapes, over the next few days I found enjoyment in not knowing what might be next. I began to trust in the guidance of the yellow scalloped shells. Feeling less fearful of getting lost, I chose to walk the fifth day on my own. The silence I experienced walking without a partner felt eerily similar to the silence I experienced at the dinner table set for one just a month earlier. Stripped of everyday distractions, conversations, and checklists, my mind wandered to places of insecurity, initially reflecting on my recent frustration with my mom's disease.

I was embarrassed by feelings that felt ugly and ungrateful. I knew I was lucky she was alive, but I was tired of being patient. Tired of hoping that one day a miracle would occur and I could get the mother I wished I had—the one that was physically present like the other moms I knew. The one that would help set up my dorm room, or come to a sorority moms' weekend, or parents' weekend. While my dad did most of that (except moms' weekend, of course, although I am sure he would have put on a wig and dressed as a mom if asked), and I was eternally grateful to him, I envied the mothers who attended events. Mom and I had a special relationship—one where I knew I could call her for advice and trust her with any information, but I was conscious of the fact that my friends didn't know who she was. To them, she was always just a character in my stories.

Out in nature, my deepest thoughts continued to unravel without permission.

Was I putting all of this pressure on myself because I was wishing for Mom to one day notice the person I had worked hard to become?

Could I value who I was as a person if I wasn't meeting my expectation of perfection?

Could I love myself for who I was without the affirmation provided by a man?

Could I ever let myself be free? To let my heart lead me like the scalloped shells did on the road?

The last thought made me pause. I was worried I wouldn't even know what it would feel like to be without fear, the need to control, or high expectations. Was it possible to just *be*?

As I processed these questions, at times even talking to myself out loud, there was something different about walking in silence on the Camino. Something that ignited an internal rumbling. Perhaps it was the rolling hills and sandy dirt under my feet—nature reminding me of the origin of creation, of my gentle soul inside. Or maybe it was having the simple task of putting one foot in front of the other each day, trusting that the arrows would lead me along the way, that allowed me to test my color-in-the-lines comfort zone. But something in my soul was moving, stirring up dust clouds like the thin puffs of ground kicked up as my feet walked along the dry gravel road.

Hard in thought, hoping to find the answers, I watched a tumbleweed roll in the distance, guided by the wind. The inanimate object rolled about as if it was doing one long chain of somersaults, like the ones I once loved to do as a child. As it joyfully danced in the wind I was reminded of how powerful something like the wind can be even though we don't see it. Which led me to think of faith.

Maybe I don't need to have all the answers, I just have to have faith and trust the wind to guide me. I wondered if I could feel light and airy, dancing in the wind like this tumbleweed. If letting go of the things that held me tightly bound—fear, control, perfection—could feel like dancing in the wind?

I walked the day's remaining seven miles wondering if I would ever truly know this feeling, or if it was even humanly possible; I imagined if it was possible, I would feel just like the tumbleweed.

◇ ◇ ◇

On our eleventh day, I woke up a little earlier than the group and walked a few streets from our hotel down to the beach, eager to set my toes free in the sand before I locked them into my sweaty socks and shoes for another twelve-mile hike.

My walk was halted after a half-mile or so when I arrived at a large rock formation that restricted tourists from traveling the beach any further. On any other beach walk, this would be my reminder to turn around and head back to homebase. To stay in the lines and venture no further. Yet, as if called by a whisper, I began to climb.

My hands and feet found natural crevices in the large grey rock that assisted my climb. Reaching the plateau, I looked down at the path I had taken from my start, tracing the line of beautiful Spanish coastal houses; the red-shingled roofs each added a pop of color in contrast to the tan sand and ocean's blue. I imagined the people who filled the houses and wondered about their stories—perhaps they were still asleep in their beds or just waking up to a warm cup of freshly-brewed coffee. I was thankful to be on this tranquil beach, to be filled up with the refreshing and reinvigorating feeling I had recently discovered being alone in nature.

Once I secured my footing, I changed my perspective to look out onto the beautiful, deep ocean. Entranced by the open abyss, I took a few steps forward, inching closer to the edge of the cliff overhanging the waves that crashed beneath. Breathing in the salty air, I unleashed my hair from its ponytail, raised my arms above my head, closed my eyes, and took in one long deep breath. Keeping my mind quiet, I inhaled another breath of air deep into my lungs, welcoming the warm feeling of the morning sun on my face and the cool breeze on my skin. The hair on my arms stood up and my entire body filled with an awakened spirit like nothing I had ever experienced before—a special kind of holy.

God was with me.

As I slowly opened my eyes, a bird soared into view. Riding the breeze, wings expanded, the bird's peace mirrored my own. With my arms stretched out, leaving my heart open wide, I saw myself in the bird—we were both evidence of creation. I envied the way it soared with ease. I wanted to fly, to feel weightless, to be free. I closed my eyes again, the gentle breeze on my face encouraging me to breathe, allowing my physical body to feel lighter. As if becoming unbound, in response to nature's calling I willingly let go. With an exhale, I released the high expectations I'd assigned myself. Released the prior relationship I was still holding on to. Released my identity as a caretaker. I let go of perfection and fear of uncertainty.

I felt alive as I inhaled confidence mixed with healing salt air, and exhaled worry and doubt. I breathed deep into the moment, knowing that when my eyes opened again, I would remain standing tall in that very place, unshaken. That I could be as light as the bird, gliding along with the wind in my wings.

Hearing only the waves crashing onto shore, I felt the whisper of comforting wisdom emanating from within:

> *Be still and know that I am God.*
> *Be still and know that I am*
> *Be still and know*
> *Be still*
> *Be.*

I felt like my body was exploding with angelic light. The kind of light I imagine that only radiates when a physical journey aligns with a soul's journey—when our outsides and insides become one.

Standing on the boulder looking out at a horizon full of endless possibility, my physical experiences on the road—pushing my legs beyond their normal capacity by walking further than I'd ever gone on a given day—reflected my inner transformation, as my thoughts, feelings, and spirit were pushed to a space they had never gone.

I often recall this moment—the feelings of charged authenticity, balance, and serenity—when I fall back into routine and rigid control, so that I remember what it feels like to live with my heart and arms wide open—to live wholeheartedly.

On the Camino, I experienced a sacred journey of my own—one that caught me by surprise. I started the journey doubting my need to search for a spiritual awakening, originally convinced the pilgrimage part wasn't for me and that the twelve-to-twenty miles of hiking a day would be an experience I could cross off my bucket list. But I ended the journey a seeker. I was awakened by the Camino, enlightened by simply following the way. Suddenly, God was no longer my childlike vision, but like the wind—a weightless presence inviting me to be my fullest self.

Twelve

I returned to Sewanee's campus for the beginning of my junior year excited by my awakening on the Camino, ready to build on my personal relationship with God. However, just as I replaced my Keens and hiking shorts with summer dresses and cowboy boots, my spiritual walks were replaced with field hockey practices, weekly games, classes, and homework. Before I knew it, I was swept back into striving for perfection and control—back into the shell of the person I was before the Camino—leaving my moments of peace and serenity as fragments of the past.

With a busier schedule I may have had less time to continue to explore my faith, but I did not have less time to think about boys. Feeling more comfortable with my newly-embraced identity as a "single girl" who could be fun and flirty, I was eager to attend parties after the field hockey season.

As if perfectly timed, our season ended the first weekend in November of 2012—the same weekend as one of the popular annual fraternity theme parties. My teammates and I pregamed together, celebrating our season, and then made our way to the party. I walked to the fraternity house with a few friends and Warren, now a Sewanee freshman and field hockey teammate, excited by what the night might have in store.

Having Warren at Sewanee made us even closer. After six years of living apart, it was fun to share similar experiences. I often visited her dorm room or would check in when we were both studying in the library. I loved hanging out with her and her friends, especially at parties. In a sense, attending college together gave us the chance to introduce each other to our newly formed selves. I no longer needed to be her protector, and she was no longer my little sister that needed protecting. Instead, I became instant best friends with the adventurous, kind, and thoughtful person she had become.

After squeezing our way through the sea of people that filled the bottom floor of the fraternity house, my friend, MK, and I found a spot in front of the stage. With the bass bumping in our ears, our bodies moved to the beat of the music. After an hour or so I scanned the dimly lit room in an attempt to find a friend we planned to meet up with. As I turned my head in a semicircular motion, like a sprinkler head slowly rotating back and forth, my eyes were met by the intimate gaze of a tall guy I had seen from time to time in my dorm. While I had never spoken a word to him, his muscular physique and confident air piqued my interest.

Our eyes locked for a moment that made my cheeks suddenly flush. Embarrassed, I immediately looked down and over at MK, "I think I just made eye contact with the cute boy-next-door," I said. Giddy, I looked back up to see if he was still there. My pattering heart simmered and an ounce of disappointment settled in when I realized my initial reaction to look down had caused me to lose him in the crowd. I shrugged my shoulders, shaking it off.

MK and I continued to dance in our prime spot in front of the stage, only to be interrupted two minutes later by a tap on the shoulder. Initially thinking it was my sister, I was caught off guard when I turned around to see the cute boy-next-door standing right in front of me with a smile on his face. "Hi," I yelled over the sound of the loud music, "I think you're cute." The minute the words left my mouth I wished I could have taken them back, ultimately humiliated by the fact that I sounded like a ten-year-old talking to her elementary school crush for the first time. Instead of turning away, he smiled, leaned over so his lips brushed my ear as he asked, "Want to dance?"

We spent the rest of the night together, our bodies entwined as we jammed to the DJ at the front of the beer-sludge dance floor.

After more of our friends joined us, I squeezed MK's hand to get her attention. "We're going to go outside to get some air," I yelled to her, nodding in the direction of the door. Weaving in and out of the crowd, I spotted Warren standing in a circle with her friends on the outside patio. Interested in what she might think about the guy I'd just met, I grabbed cute boy-next-door's hand and walked him over to where she was standing.

After hanging out with her and her friends for a bit, Warren winked at me as boy-next-door and I left to walk back to our dorm together at the end of the evening. I would learn that the cute boy-next-door's name was Alex: he was from Marietta, Georgia, and a sophomore who transferred to play basketball.

Entranced by his coy-but-cute nature, my buzzed brain had little power over my curiosity to know more about him. Pondering whether or not I should walk five doors down to my room, my quick hesitation was interrupted when his hand lightly found its way to my waist and with confidence he twisted the silver doorknob to the right and asked if I wanted to come in.

We spent the night lying in his bed, whispering in the dark like children at a sleepover, trying not to wake his suitemate next door.

Without having to yell over the music pounding in our ears, we wanted to get to know each other a little more. Alex shared that he wasn't really one to do relationships. He was a southern boy with a big family. He had confidence but wasn't looking for more, which made him mysterious but also more attractive. I was allured by the idea of creating a bit of mystery about myself as well, enjoying the rare opportunity that comes with meeting someone new to reform my narrative, choosing some stories to share and others to avoid.

I awoke the next morning with puffy eyes, my hair shooting out in all different directions from my braids, and a crick in my neck, the kind that forms when two people try to squeeze into a twin bed. I stood and whispered "good-bye" the same way we had whispered about our lives only a few hours before. Feeling a little mischievous recalling the night and how I ended up there in the first place, I tiptoed to the door, twisted the handle, and stepped into the hallway hoping no one would see me quickly walk the few doors down to my own room. I wondered if we would ever speak again. *Probably better if we didn't,* I thought, as I was intentionally trying not to get back into a relationship.

Before opening my door, I felt my phone vibrate in my pocket. I glanced at the home screen thinking it might be my roommate and it would probably be a good idea to check it before barging in. To my surprise there was a text that read "Hi" from Alex. It was an innocent text that was the start to a labyrinth—our relationship becoming more complicated than neighbors, or even friends. I wonder if he had known the baggage I avoided telling him—my parents' divorce and my mom's disease—would he still have texted me? I would find out three weeks later that while he may have played it coy, he was around to stay.

Thirteen

I finally handed in the last paper that stood in the way between me and the much needed relaxation of Thanksgiving break. All I had left to do was wait another twenty-four hours before Warren and I could board a plane back to Delaware. To celebrate, we met for coffee at the local coffee shop, Sterlings.

Something I admire about Warren is how she always has grand ideas. I, on the other hand, am more often than not the one to deconstruct her ideas with logistical challenges. As the dreamer and the realist sat sipping our coffees, warmed by our hot beverages on the brisk autumn morning, Warren's eyes lit up as she said, "What if instead of waiting another night to go home, we checked to see if there is a flight leaving tonight? Why wait when we might be able to have one more night at home?" I couldn't find much opposition to her plan. It would take a minute to coordinate everything, but at the end of the day it wouldn't be that challenging, and enjoying an extra night at home with Baird and my mom did sound nice. After a quick browse of the internet, we found a flight out of Nashville leaving that evening. The next thing we knew, our eager bodies had found their way into a car and off we went to the airport.

◇ ◇ ◇

The captain's voice rang overhead informing passengers that we would be landing shortly. I peered out of the window to see thousands of twinkling lights below, evidence of the bustling Philadelphia nightlife. As we continued to descend, the twinkling lights that once looked like stars became streetlamps, car headlights, and blinking lights atop cell towers. For an instant, the plane hovered over the runway and my body felt weightless. Clenching the armrest in preparation for what I hoped to be a graceful landing, I felt the wheels make impact with the ground and the plane bounce a few times on the runway. As the plane came to a halt, passengers bobbled around swaying slightly from side to side.

Seated toward the middle of the plane, we waited our turn to exit. I sent a text to Dad saying we had landed safely. He responded saying he and Baird had arrived with enough time to park in short-term parking; they would meet us at the bottom of the escalator by baggage claim.

Just as the plane had hovered suspended over the runway before landing, our spirits stayed elevated, excited that our plan to extend our break was successfully being executed. Warren and I exited the plane and glided through the crowds of people, weaving in and out with our rolling bags trailing behind. Eager to jump into the arms of our dad and sister, we descended the escalator and found them waiting at the bottom just as we had expected. We exchanged hugs and the traditional travel small talk regarding our flight. In turn, we asked how things were going at home since Baird had already been on break for two days. The simple response that my subconscious was hoping for, "Everything's great! We're so excited that you two are here and everyone can be together to enjoy this holiday," was not my dad's response. Instead, he paused, and in his parental "something has happened but I am going to speak really clearly in one tone so as not to cause panic" voice, he explained that Mom had gone into respiratory failure a few hours before. She and Lumlum had returned home from running errands when Mom stopped breathing. Trying to remain positive, he added that thankfully, Lumlum, who was only 110 pounds at the time, was able to call 911 and successfully provide CPR. The ambulance arrived at the scene, EMTs loaded Mom onto a stretcher, and swiftly took her away. He concluded by adding that she was still at the hospital, in stable condition. Baird, still in shock from all that she had personally witnessed earlier that day, remained silent.

Life had been running so smoothly that I didn't even think to brace for impact. Just like that, the wheels to our relaxing Thanksgiving break had touched down, but in this scenario there would be no balance. Everything had come to a crashing halt.

Instead of going home to sleep in my childhood bed at Mom's house, we slept at Beth's—of the pasta and ceiling experiment—who Dad had now been with for ten years. That night I shared a room with Warren. Baird stayed across the hall. I curled in the twin bed, staring at the light blue ceiling painted with wisps of white that looked like light fluffy clouds. Waiting for Warren to come into the room before turning out the light, I rummaged through my school backpack for a piece of paper and a pen. I desperately needed to write in order to process what was happening. Was this the moment I had been planning for since the day I found out that Mom had only a few more years to live?

At the top of my page I wrote:

> She might die. This could be it. She has never gone into respiratory arrest before. She has never just stopped breathing. This is uncharted territory, and ultimately could be the final straw.

Suddenly I realized that my carefully crafted back-up plan was rolling into action without my permission. Here we were staying with my dad in his girlfriend's house, which was much bigger than his two-bedroom garage apartment.

Was he going to take care of us now? Had he planned for this day like I had?

Mom had always said she was not going to leave this earth until my sisters and I could handle life without her. Here I was, a junior in college. I felt like whether or not I *was* ready, I *should be* ready to handle this. Warren was in college, too, and Baird was a junior in high school. We had grown so much since I was thirteen, when I first learned about the science behind her disease. Yet, no matter how much we try to prepare, the moment death stares us in the face, we learn nothing can actually prepare us.

The next morning Warren, Baird and I borrowed Dad's car and drove to the Christiana Hospital, a place we had become familiar with over time due to Mom's frequent visits. We followed the signs leading to her room, slowing as we approached the open door, a routine our younger selves regularly did so as not to wake her if she was sleeping. Reactivating the protective part ingrained in my identity—the 'Sister Superior' role that was absent a day before when Baird traumatically witnessed firsthand Mom stop breathing—I quickened my step to reach the door frame first.

Analyzing the scene we were about to walk into before my sisters' could see, I saw mom lying awake with a clear plastic tube in each nostril and another plastic tube leading from her chest to an IV machine. I quietly entered, the magnitude of her condition hitting me hard.

My chest tightened as I thought about Baird. Trying to imagine what it might have felt like to witness the traumatic chain of events that Warren and I were told secondhand. I remembered back to the first time the ambulance arrived when we were children. How scared I was of losing Mom, but feeling like I had to be brave for my sisters. It was hard not to see parallels in the experiences, only this time my little sister—her tender heart I wished to keep safe back then—was the one who was brave in the face of uncertainty.

Turning to watch Baird enter the hospital room, I noticed her shoulders ease with relief as she saw with her own eyes that Mom was still alive. There was no denying Baird's incredible growth over the years. She was no longer my cute baby sister, but was rather a strong, fearless, caretaker herself. I was suddenly in awe of her natural ability to hold it together, and I viewed her as my equal rather than a younger, more innocent one to protect.

The three of us surrounded the hospital bed. Mom's olive skin was tinted yellow and her hands and feet were blown up like balloons, something we later playfully made fun of as we all tried to make the scary situation feel light. As if hugging a glass doll, we each gently leaned in to embrace her. She told us that when she'd regained consciousness she had to ask the nurse why she was in the hospital, because the last she remembered, she was at church.

At church? I wondered, thinking it was odd that she would think she was at a place we hadn't been to in years.

Had she seen God? Had she seen the light of heaven?

I had recently read *Proof of Heaven*, by Dr. Eben Alexander, which describes his personal experience meeting and speaking with the Divine while lying in a coma. *Had Mom experienced something similar?*

I imagined Mom being transported to a unique layer beyond earth but before heaven. In this layer everything angelically glows. I imagined her sitting by herself on a pew in a beautiful church, in peace without any pain. The dialogue is inaudible, probably because I don't know her own faith well enough to know what she might say, but I envisioned a light shining down on her like a spotlight, giving her the loving attention and warmth she deserved. And then she is gone, sucked back to earth in a hospital bed, asking a nurse where she was. The thought gave me goosebumps.

Mom never really shared with us whether or not she thought she had seen God, and I have no idea if that is what she experienced, but it's what I imagined. No one pushed for more answers, we were all simply thankful she was still alive. I chose to hope that if she was in a church, and she did talk to God, she was sent back to this earth because God knew it wasn't yet her time and she still had some more life left to experience. Or perhaps, I wasn't ready for her to be gone forever and her return was God's continued gift to me.

◊ ◊ ◊

Our traumatic homecoming event sent me flying back to old habits, particularly the habit of relying on a significant other for reassurance that things would be okay. When we left the hospital, I texted Alex. In the three weeks since meeting, we'd continued talking, passing each other in the dorm hallways and around campus. We texted here and there so it felt natural to reach out to him. I let him in on the secret I had been keeping, perhaps to avoid pity I thought he might take on me if he found out my mom was sick.

In a few characters, I typed out that my mom suffered from a chronic disease and had almost died, then hit send. His lack of immediate response worried me so I tried to play it cool, hoping the news I vulnerably shared wouldn't overwhelm him. To cover any awkwardness, I attempted to lighten the mood by writing: "Bet your thanksgiving break doesn't beat that! Haha." He responded that evening, busy with his own family Thanksgiving traditions, and we spent an hour before bed exchanging texts. He, too, shared that his own family dynamics weren't perfect, making me feel less like an outsider.

"You still awake?" I whispered after I put my phone down and turned over to face Warren, lying in the twin bed three feet away. "Yes," she whispered back, and we stayed up late talking about the new butterflies I was feeling for the cute boy-next-door.

◊ ◊ ◊

Christmas vacation was like déjà vu.

Three weeks after Thanksgiving, Warren and I boarded a plane in Nashville, excited for a longer break. We waited for the wheels to connect with the runway and for the plane to come to a stop delivering us safely at the gate in Philadelphia. Just like before, we weaved in and out of the crowd, descended the escalator, saw my dad, hugged, proceeded with the travel small talk, and then another pause.

Attempting to interpret his facial expressions, I looked into his eyes, intensely trying to read his mind. He seemed to be searching for the right thing to say. On edge from the last time we landed at the airport—less than a month before—my mind jumped to the worst possible thing: something had happened again with Mom.

He looked back and forth at Warren and me (Baird had not yet returned from boarding school) and explained how his mother, whom we called 'Granny,' had passed away. It was December 14, 2012, the same day as the Sandy Hook Elementary School shooting; a day when it felt like the whole world was grieving. Though Granny had been under hospice care and we'd known time was limited, hearing that she had passed struck me with a pang of grief and surprise. Yet another break interrupted by a change in plans set me on edge. We would travel to West Virginia after Christmas for the funeral services.

◊ ◊ ◊

As I waited outside Granny's white, stucco house for the rest of the family to finish getting ready for the funeral service, I took a moment to sit with my feelings in the stillness. I knocked my shoes against the concrete step, shaking off the snow. Everything was white. Snow had covered the ground and rested upon the twig-like bushes that stood without their springtime green fluff. I felt as if I was in one of the snow globes she used to give us as kids. In an all-white winter wonderland. Memories began to flood in. The evenings as kids we spent at her house over Christmas break and New Year's. The way she would make us "Lincoln Log cabins" for breakfast—strips of toast sprinkled with cinnamon sugar stacked to form a little square.

Trying to resist the temptation to cry since I had already applied my mascara, I took a moment to envision what Granny, and her husband 'Daddo,' might have been doing together in heaven at that moment—reunited after over fifty years of marriage. I wondered if they could see me from above, a black speck surrounded by white stillness.

Just as I was thinking this, two red cardinals fluttered after each other like little lovebirds, happily dancing about. The way the birds chased each other reminded me of stories I'd heard of

Granny and Daddo in their younger years—two lovebirds at heart. I watched the birds dance about, their red feathers vibrant in the white snow. It was as if I could feel Granny and Daddo's spirits, like they weren't so far away after all. The moment was broken as my cousin opened the front door and the birds flew off. Sad to see them go, I was warmed by the reminder of the spiritual world I found in nature. The power faith can have when we believe. From this moment on I've found comfort in seeing cardinals in pairs, believing them to be my grandparents coming to check on me.

In celebration of Granny's life, my extended family spent New Year's Eve together at the luxury hotel we visited when we were young. Because Granny's house was on the resort property, we had never stayed in the hotel itself before, but I had always wondered what it would've felt like to experience the luxury of being a resort guest. Now we had a suite, and it was certainly a special way to celebrate her life and our time together as a family. We enjoyed swimming in the indoor pool and bowling like we had done as kids. While it was not the trip I had anticipated when Warren and I flew home that day in mid-December, ringing in the new year with my family became an extravagant celebration filled with champagne, fancy dresses, and a party in the hotel ballroom. The band filled the ballroom with sounds of celebration as my sisters and I took turns being twirled and dipped by Dad on the black-and-white checkered dance floor. Dad was the definition of a good time. He had a way of making even sad things, like death, feel like a celebration. It was a night to remember.

Today, I only wish I had known it would be the last time we would all be together in this way. But sometimes God works in funny ways like that. Like a divine intervention, God brings us these wonderful moments of celebration and togetherness as a gift to be cherished, knowing it will be the last.

Fourteen

A phone call can change your life.

It can offer you a job. Tell you that your friend is going into labor. Let you know you won a radio contest. But it can also be the thing we dread the most. A phone call can tell you something is terribly wrong.

I got this dreaded phone call on February 13, 2013.

I was in the Sewanee library with my friend, Samantha, just after lunch. I wasn't quite ready to get back to work, but had opened a book to try to focus my attention. My phone vibrated against the table as my uncle's name appeared on the screen. Because I was in the library and had just sat down, I felt unmotivated to go outside to pick up his call. I let it go to voicemail. If he really needed something he would leave a message and I would call him back when I left.

Not worried because it wasn't unlike him to leave a voicemail, in auto-pilot mode I unlocked my phone and clicked the triangular play button. Within listening to the first few words my casual attitude drastically changed. I instantly rose from my chair, looked at Samantha, alerting her that something was not right, and briskly walked around the corner and out the front door, phone already ringing to call my uncle back.

In a calm voice, he told me that something had happened to my dad the night before.

A stroke.

EMTs had taken him to the hospital.

I needed to come home immediately.

Immediately was the one word that rang in my head.

I was used to getting the phone call that my mom was in the hospital. But never was the call about my dad. And never was it an immediate danger.

None of it made sense.

I had spoken to Dad on the phone less than twenty-four hours before asking if he had time to help me with my summer internship applications. He mentioned he was feeling tired, but would be up to help after my classes were over the next day. I had called and left Dad a message after there was no answer only thirty minutes prior.

Was my uncle telling me that Dad didn't pick up because he was in the hospital unresponsive?

My legs collapsed underneath me and I became a tight ball on the ground, seeking any ounce of protection. Unphased by the pieces of rock protruding from the gravel sidewalk into my knees, or the fact that I lay in the middle of a commonly used walkway, I felt a light touch on my back. Samantha had come outside to check on me and rushed over when she saw me crying on the ground. Unaware of any details, she sat on the sidewalk holding me for a brief moment until my mind cleared. The word "immediately" still ringing throughout every bone in my body, I jumped up into to-do mode, a place that felt comfortable, where I knew how to excel:

Go find Warren, call Baird to check in, book a plane ticket, pack a suitcase, find someone to drive us to the airport, get on a plane, get off the plane, make sure someone can pick us up when we get off the plane.

While my body may have been moving a thousand miles a minute, my insides were nauseated, my mind numb.

What is happening?
This is not a part of my back-up plan.
This is not part of any plan.

The details of how Warren and I got on a plane so quickly are blurred, but I remember feeling incredibly thankful for our friends at Sewanee who kept our frightened bodies moving. Somehow, we made it within seven hours of the phone call to a hospital room back at Christiana hospital, the place we had been three months before. This time, instead of my mom lying in the stiff hospital bed, it was my dad's body hooked up to wires and tubes.

No. No. No. No. No. No. No. This can't be happening, I thought to myself as I inched my way to his side, hoping that in any minute he would wake up, or I would wake up from this horrible nightmare.

His eyes were closed, the tubes attached to his body keeping him alive. Over the next few hours people came in and out: doctors and nurses, my uncle (Dad's only sibling), Beth, my mom, and Baird, who finally made it home from boarding school a few hours after us. After a day of no improvement, we made the heart-wrenching decision to take Dad off life support. Though his heart was still beating, the nurses told us it would be only a matter of days, maybe hours, that he could continue living on his own.

Seated in stiff hospital chairs, my sisters and I encircled his bed. Keeping close to our hearts the hope that he could hear us, we reminisced about the past. In a quiet moment, when everyone had left the room, it was just my dad and me.

Gently placing his hand in mine, I leaned forward so that the side of my head lightly rested on his stomach. In this position, I was transported back to when I was a little girl, lovingly laughing at the fact that his jelly belly felt like a water pillow.

"Hi, Dad. It's me, Tilden," I said, as a few tears softly rolled down my face and dripped onto his hospital gown. "I love you. I want to make sure you know that. Thank you for being the best Dad a girl could ask for."

Aware that he wasn't going to be able to respond, I still listened; intensely hoping I might be able to hear the words he couldn't say, trapped in his bleeding brain. I listened to his heart beat, watching his stomach rise and fall on its own with each breath—the only signs left that he was still alive. After a few moments of stark silence, my attention was quickly drawn back to my hand as I felt the slightest movement tighten around my fingers.

"Dad? Can you hear me? Was that you?" No response or further movement. "I know you are listening. I know that was you. I am here, Dad. I love you. I will always love you."

I stared hard at our clasped hands, hoping I would see a small movement happen this time. That my mind was not playing tricks on me. But after a minute, his hand ultimately lay limp in mine. While I was disappointed, I held on tight to my belief in this miniscule movement—one last miracle packed with power. For even though the doctors warned us that it was most likely impossible for him to wake up or move, the tingling inside me fueled by the belief that he ever so slightly squeezed my hand was the reassurance I needed: that our love conquered all.

Overwhelmed with emotion, I left the room a few minutes later. I wanted to allow space for another sister to have a personal moment, but was also desperate for a breath of fresh air. I sat on the bench outside his room and wrote in the journal I'd brought in my backpack.

> At the moment Dad is without tubes, a decision that was difficult to make, but was the right thing. He is still breathing on his own. It's all a waiting game. A game where there is no winner or loser but rather just an end. An end that I am not ready for. An end that will change my life forever. My dad is the most amazing person I know. His heart is the biggest heart any man could have. He has taught me so much about being a person, how to care for people, and how to fill a room with happiness. Right now I feel as though I cannot feel. My body is moving in space while my mind and heart are on pause. I am in denial, shock, mourning, and disbelief. Not my dad.
> I will never be the same.

The following day, we arrived not knowing what to expect, but something felt off. Warren, Baird, and I found our way to his hospital room without needing to refer to the signs as our bodies had already stored the navigation in muscle memory.

Everything around me was frozen in time as soon as I entered the door. The rhythmic beeping that had been there the day before, filling the space with confirmation of life, was no longer, and a dreaded silence filled the room. The cold, sterile tile floors brought no comfort to my feet as I took a few steps closer to where the pulled-back curtain exposed the reality that I did not want to face. Overwhelmed by the uncomfortable smell, I felt as empty as the stark white walls that surrounded the lifeless body lying on the bed.

On February 15, 2013, at the age of fifty-seven, Dad was gone forever.

My dad, the person who was supposed to take care of my sisters and me if my mom died, lay lifeless on a hospital bed. The person who was meant to see me walk across the stage when I graduated from college, the person who was supposed to help move me into the city I chose to live in after graduating, the person who was supposed to walk me down the aisle and dance with me at my wedding, the person who was supposed to be "Papi" to my children. Gone.

Death happened. Loss happened. Darkness happened.

It was as if an avalanche had violently stripped me of my nicely-grown roots and rapidly dragged me to an uncharted place of loss I had never experienced before. A place of deep darkness, emptiness, and brokenness.

I walked down the long, sterile hallway leading from the hospital rooms to the cafeteria, the bright white lights blaring out any background noise. My legs somehow managed to put one foot in front of the other, guided without my soul. It was as if I was watching from above, my skeleton of a body trying its best to go through the motions. Pick up the lunch packaged in a plastic bin. Put it on the yellow tray. Walk to the cashier to pay. Find where my uncle was already sitting. Sit down in a chair next to him. Bring the food to my mouth and chew.

It was tasteless. I dropped my fork, left my food and tray, and walked quickly towards the red "exit" sign glowing above the door. Wishing I could exit my life as easily as I left the hospital cafeteria, I found a small circle of sunlight in the middle of the parking lot and sat down. I didn't care if a car needed the spot, because at that moment I needed it more. I needed the sun to warm my skin and bring my soul back to my body. I needed to find peace. I needed to feel whole.

How could this be happening?

Part Two

DARKNESS

"To go in the dark with a light is to know the light.
To know the dark, go dark. Go without sight,
and find that the dark, too, blooms and sings,
and is traveled by dark feet and dark wings."
—Wendell Berry

Fifteen

I am in a nightmare that I cannot wake up from. Everything is falling and I am not strong enough to hold up the central beams that were once my life pillars. My life that I strived to build is shattered into a million tiny pieces. My scaffolding is gone.

I can't support anyone else, let alone myself. I can't be there for my sisters, for my mom, or for any other grieving family members in the way that I want to be.

I have no control. I feel nothingness inside and yet my entire body hurts on the outside. I ache and am numb all at the same time. I feel like everything around me is foreign, I'm unable to see anything in the dark hole I can't escape.

I don't know who I am anymore, but I desperately try to hold on to any pieces I have left of my identity, to remind myself of my goals to succeed because I feel like they might help keep me afloat in the abyss where I am drowning.

I have not yet submerged because I know that is not what Dad would want for me, so I try my best to keep my head above water.

As long as my head stays above surface I know I can do it. I can keep paddling and hopefully I will get my legs back to help me kick to land. To safety. To solid ground.

I desperately seek light. To reach for the little things to be thankful for.

I am alive.

My sisters are alive.

My mom is alive.

But looking for light feels impossible when everyone around me has the dad that I don't. I must embrace these challenges to make me stronger, because I refuse to do anything else but survive. I will not let this overcome me.

And yet, all I see is Darkness.

Just like replaying a movie scene in my head, the weeks that followed my dad's sudden passing will be a time I vividly remember forever. It was a time when it was hard to breathe. A time when I would wake up and cry at nothing, because inside I felt nothing and everything at the same time.

Unlike our grandmother's formal funeral service we attended less than two months before, we honored Dad the best way we knew how—a celebration.

A testament to all the lives he touched, the tent rented for the occasion was filled to the brim with guests. Seated at the front, I turned around and let myself fully absorb the reality. The individuals sprinkled throughout, dressed in bright colors, reminded me of rainbow confetti—each pop of color ignited a feeling of joy sprinkled about in the ultimate sorrow. Dad was always the pop of color in any room, the definition of joy and light. Scanning the tent I thought, *This is how I want my life to be celebrated. It's okay to mourn, but it feels even better to celebrate. I only hope that I can fill as many hearts as he did.*

My uncle organized drummers to play since my dad loved to play and listen to bongo drums. As the drummer's hands struck the drumhead, the quick-tempoed lively pops captivated the room. The sounds bouncing about reminded me of Dad's pop of spirit. It was beautiful and heartbreaking all at one time.

◇ ◇ ◇

Feeling his presence so close in the early days after we lost him, I began to write letters to Dad in my journal. Perhaps I was trying to fill the void for the thread of texts that we would no longer exchange. Perhaps I was channeling my mom's advice shared when we were younger about writing a letter to the loved one—person or animal—who passed away. Either way, just the act of writing to my dad made me feel like he was there. Like it was one of the letters I sent to him when I was a kid at summer camp. There was

> Dear Dad,
> I am scared, sad, missing you, feeling empty, and the
> world around me feels entirely different. It is a place I
> do not recognize. But I am going to be okay.
> I love you, forever and ever.
> Love, T

something powerful about writing the words on paper. Making them permanent. I imagined him reading them over my shoulder. My first letter read:

For the next year all of my journal entries would be letters to Dad. My letters were always the words I wished I could have said to him out loud. They were notes depicting my excitement over getting inducted into my first academic honor society. About my confusion around Alex and what our relationship was and wasn't. About the expansive hole I felt deep inside that I wished would go away. About the days filled with joy, when I would feel him while standing in the warmth of the sun. Updates about my sisters, their own strength and resilience in navigating grief at such a young age. About the life we were struggling to recreate without him, but also about the journey of hope we were attempting to find, walking through it together. I imagined each word put on paper would magically lift from the page like a butterfly and fly up to the heavens, gracefully finding its way into his ear. I continue to write letters to him today as it remains our special way of connecting. A one-way form of communication that I believe keeps our spirits tethered. A critical coping tool used to navigate the Darkness I unexpectedly entered.

◇ ◇ ◇

When Dad died I was shattered. But while he was my *dad*, he was also my mom's *ex-husband*. A friend that no one allowed her to grieve because they were divorced. Mom's loss was never recognized. No one sent her cards or flowers. All of them came for my sisters and me, because he was *our* Dad. *We* were grieving. *We* had lost the second half of who created us. *We* had lost our rock—the one who was always consistent in the many storms of my mom's unpredictable health.

In the harsh storm that was this loss, I looked to cling to any-thing that would keep me afloat. Searching for comfort, normalcy, and hope, I looked to my mom. I knew she never hated Dad, as they remained good friends even after the divorce, but after being a teenager and listening to her reflect on their marriage and the frustrations of living together, I hoped enough time had passed to allow her to be the raft I was desperately seeking. The person to keep me from drowning—a mom.

But a few day after Dad's celebration of life, Mom was still behind a closed door, locking herself away to daily life and inter-actions that my sisters and I needed—the support that we required as young adults. It was as if she, too, was drifting off, lost at sea, engulfed by grief.

While we didn't know it then, the day my sisters and I lost Dad we also lost Mom. Not to pancreatitis, as we always expected, but to her unrecognized grief. The fighter's light in her diminished. After so many years of fighting her disease, she had given up. She was done being an active member on this earth. This loss in combination with previous traumas she suffered was too much.

I am not sure what hurt more: the fact that she wouldn't be there to support me when I needed her the most or the fact that I could see in her eyes she wasn't even willing to be there for herself. I never told anyone what I saw in the emptiness of her eyes. I didn't really want to believe it myself, but I was left feeling determined not to be engulfed by the same grief. I had watched her fight with admiration for so many years. I hoped she had created that same fighter in me—a sort of inexplicable resilience that was unknow-ingly pieced together within me after years of needing to bounce back from each uncertain hospital visit or phone call.

Feeling deep anguish a week later, I did what was best for me to try to reverse the powerlessness I could not escape. I couldn't protect my sisters like I did when I was twelve—the magnitude of this hurt was impossible to avoid. I didn't have the emotional capacity to put them first. I returned to what I hoped would feel like my normal life at college. In doing so, Warren and Baird did the same. Baird was only seventeen, the same age I was when Dad took me on college tours. *Who will take her on college vis-its?* I thought, panicked. Life was changing so fast for all of us. Everything was out of my control. I craved to move on as quickly as possible, to feel normal again, because home was no longer normal.

In the years following Dad's passing, my sisters and I became our own flotation device—the broken pieces of our hearts overlapping on top of each other piece by piece, holding on for dear life. We wove together what was left of ourselves to create the strongest bond, one that would keep us afloat in the nightmare that had become our reality. We were suddenly parentless.

Sixteen

Supported by the hard pew beneath me, I sat uncomfortably in Sewanee's chapel, feeling the dissonance between the burning hole of sadness in my heart and the excitement I felt to support my best friend who was about to courageously stand in front of thirty of our college peers to preach. It was her first time delivering a sermon in this formal setting, and my first time sitting in a church since my dad's celebration of life two months before.

An overwhelming silence filled All Saints' Chapel as we waited for the service to begin. I looked around in awe of the magnificent beauty of each stained-glass window. Each piece of broken glass glued together with purpose, colorfully telling stories of the Bible. The rounded arches, evidence of the late-Gothic architecture, vaulted the ceiling, ultimately creating a grandiose place for worship. I had seen this before, attending several holiday services on Sewanee's campus, but this time something felt different. The formal setting felt forced in comparison to my time on the Camino less than a year before. My relationship with God that previously evolved in nature was suddenly confined to four sandstone-colored walls.

I felt sick to my stomach and short of breath. I wondered if the person sitting next to me could hear the sound of my heartbeat getting louder and louder as my mind wandered back in time to when Dad was alive. I remembered when I was a kid, how my small hand was encased by his as we crossed the parking lot, swinging our arms back and forth as we walked towards our favorite pizza spot for a Monday night dinner. It was the same hand that I had to maneuver around mine when he lay on the hospital bed and it formed a light squeeze. The squeeze that would unfairly become our last good-bye.

Just when I'd decided to go outside for some air, my friend was invited to stand in the pulpit, so I remained seated. She approached her position with confidence and began to speak about her journey with God. She called God her protector, used language that made her faith journey seem beautiful, uncomplicated. As I continued to listen to her story, her words became muffled in the background as my own feelings of sudden anger began to roar. *How could God have such a good relationship with her but leave me in the dark? Why my dad? Why us? Why me? How could the almighty power I was taught to trust, to "let go and let God," pain me in this way?*

My heart beat faster. Each beat was like a tick of a timer counting down the moment of explosion, and I feared I might lose control. I tried to snap out of it, tried to focus my eyes and ears back on my friend who continued to eloquently fill almost every corner of the beautiful space with her allegiance to God's greatness. The only cubic feet not filled with worship was my own—my body, sitting in the third row, that was full of sudden anger and frustration.

Distracted once again by my roaring insides, my eyes locked on the rose window prominently displayed at the front of the chapel.

In an attempt to resist my feelings, I focused on the color-coordinated patterns, but within thirty seconds all the colors blurred together as I was unable to ignore the discord between what I was hearing and what I was feeling. The stark difference between my friend's experience with God and mine left me feeling hollow, and my anger slowly transformed into shame. I was angry at God for taking my dad too early. He was my rock. But in that anger I was confused, ashamed, and embarrassed.

How could someone be mad at God? Let alone how could someone be mad at God in this beautiful space where people came to worship? What kind of person was I becoming?

In the months after my dad's passing, I desperately tried to collect the broken pieces of my identity so I could glue them back together to feel myself again. Sitting in the chapel, I suddenly felt as if I had unwillingly discovered a new piece, one that had many sharp edges and large letters engraved: "God hater." I did not want this piece to be a part of me. I was not this person.

I refocused my attention on the rose window, my fists clenched as I envisioned myself throwing a boulder straight through it, shattering it, just as God had shattered me.

I blinked a few times, disrupting my focus, and realized that my friend had reclaimed her spot in the front row and the congregation bowed their heads in prayer. I quickly followed, trying to blend in with the rest of the group, hoping no one would recognize me as the fraud I suddenly felt I was.

When the service concluded, I gave my friend a huge hug, told her what a wonderful job she did, and beelined for the door. I was anxious to escape all that had just occurred. To run from this new identity marker. To run from anger and shame.

I put these feelings on lock in the pit of my stomach but the question of "why?" kept knocking at the door, my subconscious urging to get out. My mom taught us as kids that to continuously stuff your feelings deep inside just made you feel sicker, and the only way to heal was to share. I was reminded of this childhood lesson, when a week later the anger still burned and my appetite had significantly diminished to the point where I was munching on only a few carrots for dinner. I had to talk to someone. Someone who had a relationship with God, but also someone I could trust with my feelings of shame.

A few days later, I sat outside on the hard wood of a picnic bench. Across the table sat my friend who was the student body chaplain. Sitting outside of our campus coffee shop, I vulnerably shared the feelings of anger and shame I'd experienced in the chapel a week earlier. My heart began to feel lighter and lighter as I released each feeling from the depths of my insides. He told me something that transformed my understanding of my chapel experience as he looked me in the eye and said, "Tilden, your feelings of anger are okay. They are healthy. This is what God wants us to do. He wants us to have conversations with him. He *wants* us to be human. Being human means having these feelings. These feelings are meant to be had."

Suddenly, I was no longer a God-hating outsider. I was human.

My old self, the one with a foundation built of control and perfectionism, would have kept my shame hidden, never confronting my anger. My critical conversation with the chaplain shifted something in me, which made me wonder what more I'd locked up, where I had stayed within the lines of my comfort zone because it was easier to do so. What else had I ignored or said "no" to that I was actually meant to do, meant to accept rather than deny? *What did it mean to be human*? I was trying so hard to glue my original pieces back together, but maybe I was meant to create new pieces all along. To reassemble the old and the new to form who I was really meant to be.

Seventeen

I was the opposite of grounded.

Not the type of grounded my friends in elementary and middle school talked about where you were sent to your room to sit without any TV or technology. Or at least that's what I imagined since my mom never grounded us in that sense of the term. She didn't believe in it.

Mom put a strong emphasis on encouraging us to surround ourselves with people who were grounded according to the other meaning of the word—a person who was sensible and reasonable—"down to earth," as she would say. After sharing that my friend and I removed ourselves from some fourth grade drama at recess, she might have commented, "Oh, she seems grounded. That's a good friend to keep around." At the time, I wasn't really sure what made a person grounded. When I first heard Mom use the word, I pictured my friend literally standing with her feet buried in soil, as if she was a tree sprouting from the earth. But as Mom made it a personal quality to strive for, my analogy didn't seem to fit. Today, however, I have come to understand the term "grounded" to refer to a person who is one with themselves and with the world. So in my eyes, while they aren't actually planted in the ground, grounded people are rooted from within. Which brings me back to where I was as a twenty-one year old: the opposite of grounded.

I was a floating ghost of who I once was, and my restless soul refused to reenter my body. I tried to force everything to go back to the way it was months before, and was quickly angered when it didn't.

As if trying to retrace my steps to find where I had lost myself, I followed my normal routine: attending classes, sorority functions, parties. I studied at my favorite spot in the library. Forced a smile along the way to replicate what had previously felt normal, but would never be normal again. *Hadn't I learned from my parents' divorce or my mom's disease that my life wasn't normal? That I was different?* I had come to see those life changing events as things that made me stronger, a part of my story that made me who I was: self-dependent and resilient. But since Dad's passing I didn't feel any stronger or more resilient. I felt sad. Weak. Armorless. I questioned the purpose of his death, but also the purpose of my life and my identity.

One day my roommate, Karen, sent me a text. "Want to jump out of a plane with me this weekend?" If the old me—the one who stayed within the lines—was present, I probably would have quickly responded with a hard "no," but a few days later I sat with my knees scrunched up against the seat in front of me, riding in a white van packed with nine other people who had daringly said "yes."

The forty-five minute car ride and skydive safety video is all a blur. The memory becomes clear as soon as I zipped up the black jumpsuit, feeling officially locked into the experience. The skydiving leaders matched us with instructors who would be attached to us through the flight and the jump. Eyeballing based on body weight and overall stature, I was paired with a tall, skinny man who looked like he was only about five years older than my twenty-one. His long, light brown, floppy hair gave off a calming, cool vibe, and also made me kind of crush on him, making the thought of being tightly strapped to a complete stranger a little more enticing.

We were going to be sent up in pairs, and when they asked for the first group, I did not volunteer. I needed to see for my own eyes that a person could jump out of a plane and make it back alive. The minute I watched our group guinea pigs land in one piece, my arm shot up in the air to go next. I did not need more time to think, as I knew I would probably use it to talk myself out of the entire experience. My turn was now.

Pumped with adrenaline, I felt ready for anything. Hoping to feel some sort of exciting thrill that would defeat my daily feelings of emptiness, I coyly approached the small white prop plane, followed by my floppy-haired jump instructor. I was shocked the moment my eyes breached the doorway...*where were the seats?*

This experience was already totally different than how I'd imagined it. In place of normal airplane seats were two thick, solid, box-like benches. My instructor went in first and told me to sit as close as I could in front him, straddling the box seat. We faced toward the back of the plane, the side door that would open during our jump always in view. *No backing out now.*

My thoughts prior to straddling the box were consumed with the literal jump. *Would I be able to keep my legs up high enough on the landing? Would I be able to breathe? How long would we free-fall?* But no one had told me what to expect during the plane ride itself. As we ascended, the plane felt like it needed a huge gust of wind to help keep it in the air. I prayed this small white craft plane wasn't like the paper planes my friends and I used to fly in art class.

The engine continued to sputter here and there as the plane dipped up and down; with each down-beat my heart doubled in pace. I thought: I wasn't going to die jumping *out* of the plane, I was going to die *in* this plane.

Thankfully we reached the desired altitude and the side door slid open, exposing the great blue sky. I watched the other duo in the plane with us jump out first, which sparked a million more questions. I rapidly asked as many as possible in one final attempt to ensure I would do everything right. Rather than responding, my instructor—now uncomfortably strapped closely to my back—asked me to scoot forward until my body overlooked the edge of the plane. As soon as we were in position he ignored answering any of my questions and told me we would jump on three.

One.

Two.

My stomach did a flip, mirroring the feeling I always get when I do a front or back flip in water, but this time we had just back-flipped out of the plane into open air. With no time to be frustrated by the fact that he never said, "three," we were free-falling. My arms were positioned like a football goal post, stomach arched, and knees bent, my lips flapped in the wind unable to control the saliva that flew from my mouth as I tried to form a smile.

Free-falling mirrored the invisible force that grief had on my life: this strong, invisible force controlled my movements, breath, and speech. It took effort to yell a celebratory "yes" at the Go-Pro camera expertly held by my instructor. It took effort to smile. It took effort to breathe. The intense, uncomfortable pressure initial-ly caused me to feel claustrophobic, fearful that my time free-fall-ing would never come to an end. That the time my body was con-trolled by a force outside of my control would last for eternity.

After what was only about sixty seconds, but what felt like five minutes, the parachute finally opened. With a sharp yank, my body went from horizontal to vertical, feet dangling in the air. My vision cleared and I was able to take a moment to appreciate my new view in the sky. Down below I could make out the tiny white square that was the large training warehouse, surrounded by the open green fields. My instructor gave me two ropes with a rubber handle at each of the ends. If I pulled one with my right hand we would start to lean, letting the gust of wind spin us one way. Pulling the other glided us in another direction. I had been given the reins to our movements. I was in control.

I flexed my right arm and then my left, causing us to spin and swirl in the air in all different directions. My stomach enjoyed the little flutters of joy, reminding me of how I felt riding roller coasters as a kid. My body was weightless gliding back and forth in the breeze. I did not want this part of the experience to end, and yet, the ground became increasingly closer, unable to avoid. While I may have been in control of our swirls and spins, gravity remained a greater force.

Using our bodies as landing gear, when instructed, I lifted my legs as high in the air as they could comfortably go. My butt made impact with the ground, and my instructor and I glided a few more feet to a complete stop. Once I fully conceptualized that I was not dead, nor had I broken a bone, I released a yell from deep within. "That. Was. Awesome! When can I go again?"

Karen, who had yet to venture into the terrifying little plane, snapped a picture of us walking back to the group. Frozen in time is the floppy-brown-haired instructor, wearing a blue jumpsuit and carrying our red and white striped parachute a few feet behind me. I stand in the forefront of the picture, my brown hair unruly—sticking out from my ponytail in all different directions. But crazy hair does not distract from the large, wide smile on my face as I pose for the camera holding my two thumbs up. From the tip of my thumbs you can trace a diagonal line to my eyes, big and blue, open almost as wide as my grin. In my eyes there is not the deep sadness of a girl who lost her dad, but rather a fire. A spark ignited by a new inner belief.

If I can do that, then I can do anything.

I was wonderstruck thinking I might have missed out on this experience had my previous armor and controlling fear been present, back when my structured thoughts ruled my actions.

This would be the first daring "yes" I would make as the new me. Maybe she wasn't so bad after all.

Eighteen

Early in 2014, about a year into my grief, I traveled with a small group of Sewanee peers to Kingston, Jamaica. There we worked hand in hand with community members building projects for the Trench Town Culture Yard Museum. The physical act of nailing together and painting a large sign for the front of the museum mimicked my internal journey of nailing old and new pieces of my identity back together, recreating a new type of foundation. Working under the Jamaican sun I felt fueled with purpose and warmth, a feeling I longed for as I tried to rid myself of the constant cold feeling I had inside.

After I returned to Sewanee, I sought out more service experiences and learned of a Christian, short-term mission trip to Antigua, Guatemala. A whisper inside told me to apply, to say "yes" to another opportunity that took me out of my comfort zone. So, after I graduated in the spring of 2014, I headed to Antigua with the somewhat selfish hope of finding more healing glue to continue to piece myself back together, but no expectations, and no idea what I was getting myself into.

Traveling solo, I landed, passport ready in hand. Proceeding through customs, I followed the program instructions to meet the group of strangers who would become my bunkmates for the next week. Suddenly wishing we had been given dorky T-shirts to wear so we could easily identify each other, I navigated the airport trusting that there would be some sort of clue signaling who my group leader might be. Thankfully the leader's crunchy-granola, lack-of-shower look and backpack made her easy to find. We waited until all eleven members arrived—some coming from Boston, others from Greenville and Charleston, South Carolina. Some people knew each other—a pair of sisters—while others, like me, knew no one.

After exchanging somewhat awkward pleasantries, we jumped in a van and traveled forty-five miles from the airport to Antigua, where we would stay in a one-story house. Perfectly built for mission trips like these, the two large bunk rooms, two bathrooms, and one large common space with a plastic folding table for dining, a kitchenette, and a worn-in sofa would be home for the next seven days.

During our first night of worship, our group leader, Sarah, introduced a basic outline of what to expect each day. Knowing a structured daily itinerary existed provided me with comfort, though I felt intimidated by Sarah's suggestion to flow within the structure as we saw applicable, to listen to "what we were 'hearing from God.'" Sarah encouraged us also to listen to what was weighing heavily on our hearts that might interfere with hearing God's voice. She set an intention for us as well: to reflect on *why* we were called to this mission trip, confident our presence as individuals and as a group was not an accident; we all had purpose.

This question of "purpose" kept coming up as I continued to try to make sense of my dad's death. What was the purpose of him leaving this earth too early? What was my purpose, and who was I created to be? As I had just graduated, finding a career was a hot topic, and after being asked a thousand times by adults at graduation, "So, what comes next?," underneath my pleasant smile bubbled a frustration because I couldn't easily answer. If I was struggling to define who I *was*, how could I possibly know who I *wanted to be*?

Sarah's words sent vibrations through my body as I busily tried to scribble down everything she said in my journal. I resorted back to my student days when I purposefully looked busy taking notes hoping to avoid the teacher calling on me to answer a question I couldn't answer.

What did she mean by "listen to what we were hearing"? I heard the occasional moped vroom in the distance. The sound of car tires as they bounced atop the uneven cobblestone road right outside the house. The 'ting-ting' of a bike bell, probably in response to a passing hello. But what Sarah seemed to be suggesting was to listen for God's voice. This felt incredibly foreign to me. I thankfully knew just enough basic Spanish to get by on this trip, but no one had taught me to understand the language of God. *What would it sound like? What if I missed what God was trying to tell me?*

I had reservations about going on a Christian-based trip because my religious upbringing didn't include attending church regularly or reading Bible stories, something I originally associated with being "religious" or "spiritual." God and I were just establishing our relationship, testing the companionship I once felt so strongly looking out at the ocean's expanse in Spain. Our relationship was often reinforced in nature, watching creatures of the earth interact, reminding me of the intricacies of this beautifully created universe. In nature I enjoyed intently looking for a message or a sign, but I had never tried listening for conversation.

Snuggled under the crisp sheet and thin quilt provided, before closing my eyes to go to bed I wrote in my journal:

> What have I chosen to get myself into? Why am I here?

◊ ◊ ◊

The next day after dinner the twelve of us gathered around the wooden coffee table at the center of the living room. Each of us found a comfortable seat in the circle for evening worship, either on the couch or a folding plastic chair. The dim overhead light made the cream-colored walls glow a soft orange. Sarah's guitar and soft singing voice set the sacred mood.

While others closed their eyes and swayed side to side, my eyes remained open, entranced by the flicker of the candle on the center of the table, attempting to calm my initial feelings of discomfort. After she finished the first song, Sarah most likely recognized my tense body language and said we didn't have to sing along if we didn't want to. So I just listened, my face turning a light shade of pink for feeling like I'd been called out.

Why did I sign up for this trip? I don't belong here. I wanted to leave and go back to the States, but I was frustrated by feeling like the core of my being didn't belong anywhere. My mind began to wander as the music filled the room, awakening the realities I wished to keep dormant. Home would never be the same. I could no longer fit into my old skin and the more I tried, the more I failed. So, I tried to redefine "home," fundamentally shifting my view of home from a physical space to a space within my heart. To get to know the space within my heart, my insides, I came to know Darkness.

Darkness was a place of unknowns, transition, limbo. I was not who I once was, but I didn't know who I was meant to be. Darkness was full of defeat, struggle, and loss. A place of numbness. Worst of all, it was a place of solitude. An island where I was on my own. While my family was experiencing the same loss, the way we processed grief was different; and I had to process my grief alone, avoiding the feeling of shame I experienced when confronted with my inability to support my sisters the way I wanted to. The caretaker in me was unavailable.

Calling it Darkness—naming my struggles with grief that remained a year and a half after my dad passed—provided me with an ironic sense of grounding. Like a blank slate of dirt before construction, Darkness provided me with an invisible realm of "newness," a defined baseline where I could vulnerably accept and explore my grief—a place to grow and wonder. Defining Darkness made this phase feel tangible, temporary, something that I could conquer.

To quiet my discomfort during the music, I remembered the goals I wrote down on the plane ride over. Like skydriving, I had intentionally chosen to take a leap of faith, unaware of what to expect. I had to be patient.

The flickering flame began to dance—a reminder of life I saw in light—and I was taken back by the sudden noise vibrating in my throat. Hmmm. Hmmm. Hmmm. Hmmm. I softly hummed, joining in with the other voices that confidently tested their boundaries, some more comfortable than others.

Maybe this trip would be all about finding my voice in Darkness. But the self-confidence needed to activate this voice remained absent, so I continued to hum.

◇ ◇ ◇

The next evening, night two of the trip, we gathered in a similar manner. I hummed to the sound of the opening song. While we had spent the day together at a home for elders, playing games and helping out around the home, the twelve of us were still strangers who had only scraped the surface of sharing our identities.

In new situations I often take a back seat so I can observe the group dynamic and various personalities, to figure out where I might fit best. Given that, to me, these people were new, the city was new, practicing worship was new, and listening for God was very new, I felt like I was leaping from one new stepping-stone to the next, trying not to crash and burn in the lava of uneasiness I feel in unfamiliar experiences.

After the opening songs concluded, we were asked to sit in silence in order to hear what was speaking in us. The music ultimately put my mind at ease, but the listening thing still felt uncomfortable.

Following the others, I closed my eyes wondering what they might be hearing that I was missing. I adjusted my posture to sit up straight, my feet firmly on the ground and my hands lightly resting on each thigh. The stark silence was drowned out by the sound of my inner thoughts of self-doubt pestering me. *This is awkward and stupid. Why am I not hearing anything? Maybe I don't have a close enough relationship with God to hear. Maybe I am too empty, too broken to even be able to actively listen, my heart unable to telephone my faith.*

I cracked my eyes open, my eyelids hovering just above my bottom lids so I could peek, only to see everyone else still had their eyes closed. Trying to reset, I leaned back in an attempt to melt into the couch cushion, giving myself permission to become one with my new environment.

In the stillness, I listened to the sound of my breath as I inhaled and exhaled through my nose. The steady rhythm triggered a memory of the sound coming from the EKG that played in the background of my dad's hospital room; the sound that promised me there was still life until the day it no longer beeped. My chest developed a tightness that crept up my throat. The sound of my heart beat in my eardrums. There was a rumbling in the pit of my stomach begging to get out: my story that I had never fully recounted aloud, because I was scared to relive that dreaded day. I tried so hard to stomp it down, to keep my lips sealed so they would not release the words that stirred deep inside.

Inhale. Exhale.

"I would like to share something," said a voice that finally broke the silence. I opened my eyes, looked around, and realized that as everyone else's eyes slowly blinked open, they were all tracking me. It was *my* voice that tore through the fog of thoughts.

Like a shaken soda just popped open, a vulnerable, unrecognizable voice exploded with my intimate experience of losing Dad. As if in a trance, I shared my sadness, anger, and loss of grounding—my experience so far with grief. As I spoke, I began to feel my heart shining, imagining it brighter than the candle at the center of the circle, like a star-dazzling and purposeful.

After my story was over, when the out-of-body experience of words and feelings spewing from my subconscious stopped, I was shocked. I'd felt like a little girl again, uncaring of judgment. I'd allowed my soul to be free.

Brought back into my body, and recoiling from the realization of what I'd shared, a strawberry-red flush inched up my neck and face. The stark silence that followed was like a hand choking me. I was frightened I had let my soul run too far, had said too much. I needed someone to say something.

Had I said the wrong thing? Or spoken out of turn? If only the phrase "eat your words" was not just an idiom!

Following the pause that felt eternal but must have only been a few seconds, a middle-aged woman with short brown hair began to share about a time in her life where she struggled with her self-confidence, ultimately leading to self-harm. Like a ripple effect, person after person began sharing large, vulnerable pieces of themselves. By the end of the night we were no longer strangers; we were bravely connected by our deepest truths—our humanity—and it had started with me. With my voice.

Was I hearing God?

Was my inability to hold in what I selfishly wanted to all because God was deeply calling me to share?

Was this my purpose on the trip—to break down my walls so that others felt comfortable doing so too?

Maybe I could hear God after all.

I had difficulty going to bed—my whole body felt fueled by wandering thoughts as I replayed what had happened an hour earlier. I desperately wanted to further articulate what I had just been a part of. To grasp the power of vulnerability I witnessed sitting around the small flickering flame. It was like trying to understand the underpinnings of magic.

There was something powerful about speaking my truth—in responding to the rumbling inside—that allowed us as a group to connect in our places of pain, in our experiences of realness in their most pure form. Through the release of pain, we were transformed on both a tangible and intangible level. Our stories, daringly shared, connected us in a deeper way than I had been connected with some people I had known for a decade. The act of sharing—of radical transparency—had ultimately bred community.

Prominent in my memory of that night is that while owning the pieces in us—those that were painful—the air in the room felt the opposite. Rather than feeling heavy—filled with shame, sadness, or grief—the energy of the room softly glowed like the small orange flame still burning in the middle of our circle. In sharing our points of pain we configured a space of authenticity, of truth, of light—where we realized our pain was not just our own.

Tucked under my sheet that night I smiled, feeling as though I had found a glimmer of light in my Darkness. It was as if God had a spotlight, like those used to illuminate an actor or actress on stage, and it was pointing at me. I felt chosen. For the first time, I wholeheartedly felt that I may have a powerful gift. Like I might be a critical player in building community, and creating space for others to be acknowledged and seen for their own, hard truths.

My soul vibrated with the same full-body feeling I experience when I'm anxious, but this time, rather than feeling like I couldn't breathe, I felt like I could literally jump off the ground and fly. There was the beginnings of a whisper telling me, showing me, that I wasn't ordinary, I was extraordinary—we all are.

While my entire body glowed with warmth, I finally closed my eyes and drifted off to sleep, feeling as though unlocked deep inside of me were the kindlings of the power and purpose I needed to reclaim my life.

◊ ◊ ◊

Empowered by the previous night's calling, I was eager to do some more listening in a place where I'd felt God's spirit from the beginning—nature. I walked outside, toes tickled by the soft grass, opened the flaps of the hammock strapped between two thin trees, and wiggled around to find a comfortable seat cocooned by the colorful cotton threads.

I admired the volcano off in the distance, in awe of its natural beauty. There was something jaw dropping about viewing what

I had only seen in pictures. From the outside, the volcano stood powerful and majestic, the majority of its base covered by lush, soft green until its rocky brown peak. Though unable to view the inside, I imagined the active rumbling of magma mimicking my churning insides from the night before.

I closed my eyes, feeling warmed by the morning sun on my face. *What else was God telling me that I had not been able to hear?*

As I blinked my eyes open, a lone red flower grabbed my attention. The green stem effortlessly swayed in the breeze, but the roots remained unhinged. When it was still, the flower soaked up the warm rays of sun, the same rays I felt on my face. Later this flower would most likely feel reinvigorated by the afternoon rain showers Guatemala experienced during this time in June. This flower was a reminder of the sacred and divine creation of life itself.

Entranced by this idea of divine creation, I lay back in the hammock so I could look up at the sky. The cloudless blue expanse acted as a blank canvas for further meaning-making.

Sometimes emotions stirring in my soul are too new or too powerful, and I struggle for the language to explain the inner knowing. As a kid, when I didn't have the language to outwardly process the rawness of life in a given moment, I would resort to trying to understand it through metaphors.

In a similar manner, enamored by the complexity of creation wrapped up in the simplicity of the flower standing before me, I wondered, what if I was like a flower: before my dad passed, I had roots deeply entrenched in the ground that was my environment, nourished by my parents, friends, and confidence-growing experiences of my childhood. I was blooming in the comfort of Sewanee's domain. When Dad was suddenly taken from this earth, my firm foundation was uprooted like a plant viciously pulled out of the ground. I lived dangling out of the soil for weeks, anxiously reaching to find comfort, hope, and happiness, but it wasn't until my new foundation started to be built that I was able to be replanted. My new foundation—the things that made up my new soil—seemed to be built through recent experiences where I said "yes," like skydiving, traveling to Guatemala, and growing my relationship with God.

Following this metaphor, I wondered, *what, then, comes next?* Perhaps God was telling me I still needed to grow, to rebloom. And like a flower that follows the sun, maybe I needed to allow myself to be guided by my heart; by the times where I felt warm, whole, and alive. Just like trusting the yellow shells and arrows to show me the way when walking the Camino, maybe I needed to surrender to my heart, trusting that it would lead me to *my* way; the way created just for me.

Good thing I was in a place that encouraged us to listen.

Nineteen

Strong vibrations shook my body as if someone was viciously shaking the posts of my bunk bed. To my dismay, the vibrations were not made by a group member pulling a prank on me, but by a small earthquake that shook our entire room, startling everyone awake the next morning. Like the sound of my phone vibrating against the bedside table when it's time to wake up, the shaking of the earth's surface seemed like God's alarm clock, forcing me to get out of bed to complete the important work that needed to be done.

Eager to do more listening, I wondered what this morning's wake-up call might suggest about our day. The plan was to visit Potter's House, a Christ-centered organization empowering and supporting people living in Guatemala City's trash dump.

The Guatemala City dump is the largest landfill in Central America, receiving over a third of the country's trash. The scavengers, whom Potter's House refers to as "Treasures," reside in the dump where they compete for various items they can recycle and resell. The organization encourages the Treasures to find confidence beyond the garbage; its mission is to fight poverty in Guatemala by providing holistic development programs and promoting a personal relationship with God. As volunteers—referred to as servants—walk around the landfill community in small groups, they are guided by the curriculum provided.

Before visiting the first home, the group leader walked us through a typical home visit. I repeated the four steps in my head so I wouldn't forget: "Provide a friendly greeting, introduce the members of our group, share that God loves them, and pray." For visiting volunteer groups, the leaders of Potter's House created an easy-to-remember acronym to keep conversation flowing: B.L.E.S.S.

Body: How is the person and/or family's physical health?
Labor: How is work going? Is there anyone in the home that goes to school?
Emotions: How is everyone in the home feeling emotionally?
Social: How are relationships in the community? Does the person have any friends or family close by to provide support?
Spiritual: How is the person's relationship with God?

At the end of the visit, we would provide the family with a bag of food. For someone who was not fluent in Spanish or prayer, I appreciated the suggested instructions to guide my interactions with the Treasures. But the impending visits made me nervous. In this new environment I was worried about stepping out of bounds and asking the wrong question or praying for the wrong things. I was just starting to deepen my own faith—to feel from within that God saw me, that there might be a greater purpose to my story. I didn't feel like I—a foreign stranger—had the right to teach when I was learning myself.

Walking from the community center to the first home, it became clear to me that the Treasures lived in deep poverty. Their shelters were made of scavenged materials and trash was sprinkled like wildflowers back home. Walking through the narrow dirt pathways, I held tightly to the ripped piece of paper where I'd scribbled notes.

Just follow the instructions, I told myself. *You can overcome your fears of saying or doing the wrong thing in order to serve this community.*

Once we arrived at the first house—a small rectangular space created by large tin sheets, metal gates, and a dusty tarp—I froze. I was right back in my elementary school classroom, unable to speak up, unwilling to share because I was too scared of having all eyes on me and being wrong. Another member of the group, fluent in Spanish and natural at leading worship, broke the silence. Without glancing at her notes, she masterfully ran through B.L.E.S.S. and prayed for the man who shared that he was struggling to find work. His family had left and he was living alone, begging for God's grace. I watched in awe of the man's vulnerability to share so easily with our small group—a circle of total strangers. I moved from house to house, my emotions fragile from the Treasures' honesty and suffering, my sensitivity charged.

◇ ◇ ◇

After Dad died, I actively processed varied degrees of sadness, anger, confusion, and frustration: my friends around me at college had dads, and I didn't. And really, for most of my life these feelings stirred inside as I looked around at friends who had healthy moms and married parents. A part of my identity, whether or not I recognized it at the time, was always striving to be *more*, perhaps to make up for what I thought I lacked.

The Guatemala City dump—a place where people lived—with the absence of greenery, of running water, of available work and food, of things I took for granted on an everyday basis, challenged feelings of my own Darkness. It was hard not to compare levels of suffering. I had lost my dad, but I felt like these individuals were living with the loss of so much more. And yet, the people I met were truly *treasures*—their resilience burning bright amongst the mounds of rubble. With each home visit I remained in my comfort zone, standing silent in the back as I witnessed the Treasures vulnerably proclaim confident trust in God when it seemed like everything was stacked against them.

Towards the end of the day we walked into one of our last homes. Similar to other shelters in the dump, it was constructed of large tin rectangles held together with a few screws and positioned on the edge of a heaping garbage pile. This dwelling had a little more open space, making it hard for me to hide in the background. A petite woman welcomed us into a room that appeared to be the kitchen, bedroom, and living room all in one. The short woman, her hair woven in one long braid that draped down the middle of her back, and her sister, also tiny, looked at us expectantly, waiting for someone to say something. I intensely stared at the dirt floor. My gaze ultimately found a spot on the colorful woven mat made of recycled plastic, trying to ignore any eyes that might suggest it was my turn to speak.

Escaping the role of facilitator once more, I relaxed and looked up. The woman's eyes locked with mine as she began to share in Spanish that she was having a hard time taking care of her family because many of them were sick. As I attempted to silently translate what she was saying, she explained how she was trying so hard to be strong, but as soon as she said it out loud her bottom lip began to tremble, her shoulders slouched, and she began to cry.

I knew that feeling. What it felt like to struggle to care for everyone. What it felt like to try so hard to be strong for so long, only to hit a breaking point when you can't be strong anymore. To cave in with shame as a result of not being the person you believe your family needs you to be.

Just like the night when I felt God ignite a fire in me to speak, I felt a sudden urge to be with this woman. To let her know she was allowed to break down, allowed to cry. She was allowed to be human, and her vulnerability made her beautiful.

Unconcerned about whether it was the right or wrong thing to do, my voice broke the silence as I asked her if it would be alright if I held her hand. She nodded and before I was fully aware of what was happening, I moved right next to her and held both her hands in mine, determined to pour every ounce of strength and love I had from my hands into her soul. My eyes formed tears as I was moved by the feeling that, all our differences aside, we had become one. *I see you*, I tried to silently communicate with my eyes staring deeply into hers. *You are worthy. Your story is worthy, and you are seen.*

Feeling something touch me, I looked over to see one of my group member's hands resting lightly on my shoulder. Another group member then placed a hand on hers. Within a few seconds we were closely knit within the small space the woman called home. Like an IV sending nutrients into her veins, we were connected, infusing this woman with strength and love. While we couldn't provide her physically with more than a bag of food—a resource that would contribute to serving her basic needs for probably no more than two days—we were doing something even more powerful. We were surrounding her with the greatest force God gives all human beings: *love*. Despite lack of access to running water or electricity, we were sustaining her with the power of love.

Sarah pulled me aside after we left the dwelling, and I braced myself for the potential criticism due to breaking the B.L.E.S.S protocols. Instead she said, "Did you see what just happened in there? The healing aura we were able to create which stemmed from authentic connection and love? That was because of *you*. The Lord was speaking through you. I hope you continue to listen."

Whoa, is the only thing I remember thinking, completely flabbergasted by the empowering moment that happened, once again, all too quickly.

On the van ride home when I had more quiet time to process all that I experienced, I journaled about how my day started with the earthquake—God's wake up call. Then, as the day moved on, my own fears of not getting it perfect distracted me from truly showing up, ultimately drowning out any divine messages. And yet, I learned from the Treasures' vulnerability and openness. Where the petite woman experienced Darkness—the chapters of her story filled with sickness and hardship—I saw Light. The honest sharing of her pain generated a community of love and light. A connection of hearts that had also known hurt.

I clasped my hands together, recalling the feeling of her hands in mine. I felt free from the walls that were holding me back. My actions were led by my heart, captivated by her truth, and ultimately unconcerned by potential judgment. I will never forget the warmth that radiated inside of me as a result of seeing myself in her. And while I didn't have time to share a piece of me with the woman, I looked into her eyes hoping she could sense the pain in my own story, so she could know she was not alone. I *felt* her pain, but I also was mesmerized by her incredible beauty. This woman had known heartbreak, hardship, and sadness. But she also knew the most pure form of strength: vulnerability. In a place I least expected, surrounded by acres of trash, I witnessed true beauty.

It was my first introduction to being *real*, when we open our hearts and boldly expose our scars.

In the crevice that was the Guatemala City dump, I had never felt more alive. There, critical shift occurred in my own under-standing of self: perhaps I was never meant to be left completely broken, but rather, made into something more beautiful and alive.

◇ ◇ ◇

On our final night together, our group dined in celebration of our work over the week, sharing reflections of our most mean-ingful moments of the experience. After dinner we gathered in the living room and Sarah began to play her guitar to a melody I recognized from the previous night.

I thought back to the question of intention set on the first day: *Why was I on this trip? What was my purpose?*

My experience in Antigua was so much more than a mission trip for me. In just one week my broken heart had glowed more purely than it ever had before, fueled by the power of vulnerable human connection. I thought about the woman in the city dump, how badly I wanted her to know that her soul was seen for some-thing more than its heavy pain. That she was extraordinary, her resilience stronger than anyone I knew. Her humanity—the pain, beauty, and truth—was acknowledged.

Then, I heard a whisper, *that is what I see in you.* The music of worship became a muffled noise in the background. *I see you,* a divine whisper inside continued, *your pain, your beauty.* The hairs on my arms stood up, chilled by what I felt whispering deep within.

Is my observation of the woman how God is seeing me? Is God telling me what I didn't have time to share with the woman—that we are all evidence of extraordinary creation?

Maybe my purpose on this trip all along was to discover the

true, raw beauty of life, something that seemed to be revealed only to those who had known brokenness.

Ironically, in feeling shattered—experiencing Darkness—I'd been exposed to the most pure forms of light and love, and witnessed the power that authentic human connection has to heal the most vulnerable hearts. My own vulnerable heart no longer felt like punishment, but a superpower. A gift.

Unable to hold back a smile, I joined with the others in song. This time, rather than keeping my lips locked in a timid hum, I opened my mouth wide and let my heart sing.

Twenty

Like dew freezing flowers in the first frost, my resilient soft-ness gained in Guatemala hardened when I returned to the States. My tender moments of intimate connectedness in the trenches of the dump were replaced with the hustle and bustle of to-do lists, material goods, and societal pressures I felt to find a job, move to a new city, and begin my career in the real world. The tunes of inspirational, healing melodies were replaced with networking phone calls and interviews. The call to listen I heard so clearly only a few weeks before was drowned out by the pressure to procure a high paying, respectable job in a big city. I felt American culture forcing me to assimilate back to old habits—a place I now wasn't sure I wanted to go.

While eager to see what life outside of school would be all about, I was apprehensive about leaving the comfort found in the predictability of education—a world I knew how to easily nav-igate. To get As and Bs, I had to submit assignments and work hard. To be captain of my field hockey team, I had to demonstrate leadership and practice my skills every day on the field after school. There was a clear path in everything—academics, sports, advancing to the next grade level. I thrived in this structured and social space. I was worried I wouldn't have enough strength to handle the series of unknowns that inevitably comes with entering the "real world." I suddenly felt like I was staring at a blank canvas.

Where should I move?

What jobs should I apply for?

Where are my friends living?

As adults liked to remind me: *the world was my oyster*. But having so many new options reminded me of being a kid, when I would spend fifteen minutes staring at the Walgreens' checkout counter candy bars, having a hard time choosing a special treat. There were almost too many options. Too many decisions to be made. Too many times I could make the wrong choice and fail.

I knew I didn't want to stay in Delaware. Memories of adventures with Dad were too hard to confront, and Mom's mental and physical health hadn't improved. After being away from home for over eight years I realized being too close was unhealthy for my personal development. I liked pretending everything was fine, that her disease didn't exist, which was easy to do just catching up over the phone from time to time.

I ended up deciding to move to Washington, D.C. I figured I needed to just pick a place and go, not open myself up to too many ideas. Several of my friends moved there after graduation, and if Mom's condition worsened, it was less than a two-hour train from home, so it seemed like a plausible first start.

I moved into a three-story townhouse in Glover Park, a popular spot for young grads, with five other girls. Without a job, I asked to have the smallest room so I could pay the lowest rent. It wasn't until I moved in that I realized that when living with six people in one house, the smallest room essentially is a closet. It could fit a full-size bed, a dresser, a small circular rug, and, thankfully, a small closet. While small, it would become my nook, a place I felt safe returning to after a long day at the internship I was offered a few weeks after moving.

Looking for my first job I felt pressure to find the *best* job. Not the best job for me, but the job I assumed society would deem fabulous. Living in D.C., I felt I had to basically be the president. Everyone was so focused on what you "did" that it seemed like your job defined you. While asking what someone does for a living can be a logical conversation starter, there was something about being in this city that made the question feel political. Whether I was at a bar, on the bus, or in an Uber, strangers and new acquaintances seemed solely interested in status. One time when I was asked the question by an Uber driver, I told him that I was the White House florist just for fun. I swear his demeanor slightly shifted, altering his customer service just enough to make me feel like I had suddenly jumped from being a twenty-three-year-old nobody to a political princess.

Facing my blank canvas of post-college life, I figured I could try out anything. I applied for assistant jobs at law firms—though I had no background in law—because working for an important lawyer seemed to be something cool I could say. With a degree in International and Global Studies from a liberal arts college, I applied for jobs at UNICEF and other well-known international organizations. I even submitted my resume for an entry-level position with the United Nations. As a result, I spent weeks frustrated and in tears over not getting a job offer. I wanted my credentials—everything I had worked hard for in college—to be enough for an organization to consider me, but I soon realized that a single piece of paper boasting my education and recent camp counselor experience would not get me in the doors I thought I needed to open in order to be considered a success.

Finally, thanks to a chain of networking and informational interviews, I landed an interview at a bipartisan think tank. I cried after my interview because, when asked, I could not recall the name of the president of China (something I will now never forget). Thinking I had totally botched yet another interview, I was shocked to receive an email offering an internship in the Director's Office. Unsure if it was because they saw potential in me or because my connection to the organization had enough pull to get me the position, I was thankful, nonetheless, to have my first job in my new city. Getting my first real offer felt like getting the first college acceptance letter. After weeks of trying to find my place in the real world, I finally felt accepted.

◇ ◇ ◇

I woke up each morning and put on my fitted pencil skirt and blazer—items I thought were needed to look the part of being a "somebody" in D.C. Influenced by *The Devil Wears Prada* high-status picture of success, I kept a pair of heels in my desk drawer, ready for whenever a visitor or the President & CEO was in the office. After several weeks, instead of using my college education for research or implementation of creative projects, I became someone who would bend over backwards to make sure all managerial requests were answered. If food was needed for an event, I would order it. If an email needed to be sent on behalf of the CEO, I would help send it. I was an assistant to the assistant, and success in the role was determined by never saying "no."

One time I was asked to get a cell phone case for the CEO's new iPhone. A few minutes later I found myself walking across the city in high heels to the nearest Verizon store in eighty-five degree heat. College didn't teach me to buy *two* cases during that trip in order to give the CEO a choice, since apparently coming back with one was simply unacceptable. She was ultimately disappointed by my purchase of the standard, black hardcover case. So, back I went to the store, heels clopping on the cement and a blister forming on my left ankle, to purchase another case for comparison, and then back again a third time to return the one she decided not to keep. Somewhere along the way I began to wonder if this job was the right one for me, questioning if it was worth working in a job I didn't love just to meet cultural standards.

Was this the person I wanted to become? My Type A personality told me that if I wanted to be an assistant, I would do whatever it took to be the best assistant. But did I really want to walk to phone stores or book plane tickets for a career? *Was this my purpose?*

One minute I felt I fit in and the next minute I felt I was losing myself. I wanted so badly to see the road map of my life. I liked to imagine a bookshelf of old scrolls, like the ones shown in history movies, each containing a person's life path fully sketched out; I so desperately wished I could peek at mine, unveiling the path that lay ahead.

Would doing this work guide me to my greater purpose and I just had to bite my tongue and hang in there? My time on the Camino and in Antigua had fueled my faith to follow my heart's lead, listening to a divine whisper within. But listening was becoming impossible as it was harder and harder to hear over the loud noise of everyday life.

◇ ◇ ◇

Wondering if my job was the right fit wasn't the only big question I was confronting at the time. While I was trying to uncover my purpose, I was also trying to understand my feelings around Alex. After losing Dad, our relationship continued to be complicated for the remainder of my junior and senior years. There were many times when his arms stopped me from completely crumbling to the ground or provided the warmth I needed to keep my soul alive. But there were other times when I was overly frustrated because the person he said he loved wasn't the same person I knew, this new me that was created involuntarily after Dad died. *How can he love me when I don't even love myself?*

My soul needed space—personal quality time to find myself without the pressures of a relationship or the feeling I was constantly letting him down. But my heart needed to be loved, to be held. So for a year and a half Alex patiently rode in the passenger seat of my emotional roller coaster until I graduated from college, which felt like a natural break for both of us to go our separate ways. I always thought by breaking up I was releasing him of *his* caretaker duty; our breakup would be what he actually wanted but never had the heart to say to me, knowing I couldn't take another heartbreak. But that was never the case.

Just as Alex came into my life when I didn't want a relationship and wasn't ready for one, and stayed though I often kept him at a distance, he continued to somehow maneuver his way through the walls I put up. He never gave up on us.

Alex and I officially broke up in May of 2014. A month before Guatemala, three months before I moved to D.C. After the breakup, I often questioned if something was wrong with me. If my heart was too broken, too consumed with grief, to ever love again.

Alex also spent the summer as an intern in D.C. and we saw each other a few times after I returned from Guatemala, respecting the close friendship we developed. There was something about Alex that I was unable to deny, a deep connection and appreciation tying us together.

On his last night in D.C. before returning to Sewanee, we went to dinner as "friends." He'd parked his car outside my townhouse and after dinner we walked home, approaching his car slowly, and with it, we stared down the moment we had tried to avoid the entire night. We would not be returning to campus together. It was time to officially say good-bye.

Already warmed by the summer humidity, he leaned back against the trunk of his car and held my hands in his. Taking one more moment to avoid this inevitable conversation, I looked up at the night sky. A few bright stars peered through the soft white clouds while others remained invisible, hidden because of the nearby streetlights and the D.C. urban light.

While I can't remember exactly what he said—we could make things work, this doesn't have to be the end—I remember looking into his eyes and thinking, *this is literally the most perfect guy.* In the two years we had known each other, his actions and words had shown me how strong his love could be. How willing he would be to "go to the end of this earth" for me, something my mom had always promoted as a sign of true love. It was a love I knew I deserved. All I wanted to do was to fall into his arms and surrender to it. And yet, I felt nothing. I was consumed with panic, wondering if I would ever be able to love again.

Am I supposed to be with Alex and I just keep pushing him away?

I didn't have the answers, so I said good-bye, reassuring him we were making the right decision. It was time for us to go our own ways, even if it felt hard letting go. My hand reinforced my words as I squeezed his one last time before releasing it and walking away.

I reached my front door and turned around before twisting the doorknob to go inside. Perhaps I looked back because I wondered what might happen if I ran down the walkway and leapt into his arms. Wondered what life might look like if I told him to wait for me. That we could make this work, I just needed time. Or maybe, I turned hoping that if I saw him get in his car to drive away I would feel more confident in my choice to cut all ties. Instead, I watched him get into his car and drive away, acknowledging that with each goodbye we were only making things harder on our hearts.

I climbed the stairs up to my bedroom and collapsed on the bed, face forward into my pillow, defeated. Fear lingered as I wondered if I was making the wrong decision. I prayed my love was like the stars above us. Something I knew was there, but concealed by my remaining fog of grief. Similar to how a power outage could unveil the twinkling of all the stars, I wondered what strong force was needed to reignite the love within my heart so it could twinkle for someone else.

I was trying to trust in the whisper I'd recently discovered stirring inside. The soft rumbling that I imagined guiding me down the path I was meant to forge. But setting an intention to listen was much easier said than done. Externally, I felt I was doing everything right. I successfully moved to D.C. and landed a job at a respected think tank. I wore pencil skirts, blazers, and a cute pair of black heels. I was trying to move beyond my feelings of grief in order to redefine my new normal that was grounded in routine. Yet, internally, I remained unsatisfied.

Twenty-One

Every morning I took the 33 bus from Glover Park to Federal Triangle to get to work. One morning I stood at the bus stop a little earlier than normal so I could get to work in time for an event, greeted by the morning sun beginning to peer over the city skyline. Boarding the bus, I popped my earbuds in and listened to a *Serial* podcast episode. I loved these early mornings when it felt like the world was just waking up, significantly less people on the streets than at eight a.m.

As the bus glided down Wisconsin Avenue, I watched the outside world go by. Per usual, I passed all the shops in Georgetown, their signs reading "closed," and continued onto M street, only a few pedestrians and morning runners sprinkled about.

Each side street passed quickly, but in one, a congregation of people experiencing homelessness sitting outside a brick building caught my attention. Thick grey blankets wrapped around bodies huddled together. The group was too far away for me to make out what was happening, or what they might be waiting for, if they were waiting for anything at all.

My thoughts shifted from the detailed *Serial* case to the Treasures I met in Guatemala. People who, like this group of people, were living in poverty. They reminded me of the woman I connected with in her home—of her pain and of my own hurt knowing that I couldn't remove her burdens. But I also remembered the intense interconnectedness I felt holding her hand in mine—evidence of the power of human connection and the miracle of love.

Something about this group of people burned in my heart. A feeling I couldn't shake. Something telling me to do more. As soon as I got to my office I googled "homeless shelter Foggy Bottom." The first thing that appeared was information for Miriam's Kitchen, a non-profit organization with a mission to end chronic homelessness. After reading more about the organization, I instinctively clicked "Volunteer" and filled out an application to serve breakfast before work.

Every two weeks I woke up at 5:30 a.m. to help prepare fresh eggs, berries, and breakfast meats to serve to clients who lined up for a warm morning meal. When tasked with cooking eggs, I would hold each egg for just a second and pray over it, *Please bring warmth to the soul that devours you.* Then the next one, *Please bring joy*, and the next, *Please bring comfort.* Breaking each egg, I plopped it on the griddle, hoping that my prayers for comfort and joy would scramble together like the egg yolks. Eggs served with salt and pepper and a little extra love.

Being in the same space as the homeless guests allowed me to feel comfortable—less alone. Since Dad's death, reconnecting with peers was sometimes a challenge. While their intentions were always thoughtful and caring, a feeling of frustration lingered. At twenty-three, the majority of my friends hadn't experienced losing a parent. Their support was comforting, but they didn't actually *know* what it felt like to live in the Darkness—to be swallowed by grief. They weren't able to fully understand how everyday conversations felt flimsy in comparison to the deeper, more meaningful conversations I yearned to have—conversations around loss, brokenness, and healing. I was searching to be surrounded by people who had known similar heartbreak.

While I had the privilege of having a roof over my head and my basic needs met, as a volunteer, I felt a unique sense of belonging in a space filled by others who understood my underlying ache, even if it may have been caused by something different. While every day that I volunteered was a special day, the mornings I was asked to help on the serving line were even more meaningful. The opportunity to serve filled a hole in my heart I couldn't confirm existed until I felt the energy I received when greeting guests with a pleasant "good morning" and smile.

Naturally some folks were more chatty than others, but I was intent on looking each of them in their eyes, as if to say, *I see you,* acknowledging their humanity. I only wished I had the time to sit with them to fully learn their story. But in the thirty seconds I scooped fruit onto guests' trays, while they did not know it, the feeling was reciprocated. Like a mirror, in acknowledging them for their humanity, I felt like I was seeing myself, or becoming a little more like the person I wanted to be. I wondered if this was what my yoga instructor meant, when she ended her class saying, "the light in me honors the light in you. Namaste." While I may have been on the serving side, each set of eyes I looked into looked back at me and served me with the spark I needed to further ignite my purpose, the flame required to gather my bearings in the Darkness.

The light radiating from my insides became clouded the minute I stepped into the office for my internship. The bathroom stall on the bottom floor where I changed my clothes became a portal where I stepped into a different skin, slipping out of my sneakers and athletic shorts and into my professional attire. I had envisioned fitting into this high-class, successful environment for most of my adolescence and early adulthood, but suddenly my new outfit felt like a costume—colorless and robotic, as if I was simply going through the motions. The drastic contrast between how my soul felt in the two different environments was a clear sign I couldn't ignore. If I was trying to listen, this seemed to be enough of a sign that I should not be working at the think tank.

Perhaps life was not about waiting for the large signs, but rather making smaller choices that knit together purpose. Finding Miriam's Kitchen that day on the bus was meant to happen in order to fully illuminate what I had been shown in Jamaica and Guatemala—there was more in store for me than what I'd originally limited myself to, and it had to do with human connection, not computer screens. Like constellations in the sky, my service experiences were like stars sprinkled into my life's chapters, almost dimmed by my understanding of success. But I felt it loud and clear. It was time for me to stop following the droning sounds of societal norms and finally connect the brightened stars; the image unveiled meant to illuminate the dark sky—it was always about people.

Just as I googled to find Miriam's Kitchen, after a rabbit hole of googling various service organizations, I stumbled upon my next pivotal building block in reassembling my identity: City Year.

◇ ◇ ◇

After only a year of my internship, in the summer of 2015 I eagerly traded professional wear for baggy khakis, black sneakers, and a red City Year bomber jacket.

City Year is an AmeriCorps program that helps thousands of

public school students nationwide reach their full potential. Many of the students live in a systemically under-resourced community where external factors can make it hard for them to come to school ready to learn every day. During the service year, each AmeriCorps City Year member is assigned a partnering school with a team of other members to support the whole school and as individual classroom initiatives. The role of the Corps member within schools is to cultivate positive relationships, support academics in addition to social emotional learning, and enhance belonging and engagement for students.

I turned twenty-four in July, trained over the summer, and in August I recieved my assignment: a second grade classroom in a K-5 elementary school in Southeast D.C.

My morning commute would start three hours earlier than my intern commute and last thirty minutes longer. I'd travel from D.C.'s Northwest corridor to the Southeast, a place my friends living in Glover Park rarely ventured.

In City Year fashion, my team and I cheered, sang, hooted and hollered, celebrating each student who entered the school building on his or her first day. My team of eighteen, the largest team assigned to one school, brought the energy in song. While we all received extensive training prior to school starting, my first day jitters were like fireflies in a jar, bustling about.

The first time I stepped into my second grade classroom, a hush went over the class. Twenty-three sets of eyes stared at me, curious about my existence.

"Good morning," I said, quickly contemplating what I would like them to call me. "My name is Ms. T. I'll be your City Year Corps Member this year."

A little boy, wearing the school uniform—khakis, like my own, and a green school T-shirt—raised his arm into the air and waved. "Hey, Ms. T!" he said, followed by a wide smile. I smiled back, feeling reassured this was where I was meant to be.

While it took some time getting used to, Ms. T would become the identity of the new person I was just beginning to know when I left Guatemala. A person who found greater healing in the twenty-three hearts sitting at their tables right in front of me.

The teacher, Ms. Hope, redirected the students' attention and our first day of learning began.

◇ ◇ ◇

Ms. Hope stood at the front of the classroom with her hand up, enthusiastically tapping her fingers against her thumb as she sounded out words for the daily phonics lesson. This technique of tapping was new to me, a way of learning that was not taught when I was in second grade back in the '90s. Just like the students, I had to follow along in order to get the hang of the new Fundations model. With one hand up, students mirrored the teacher sounding out each word. Each sound was made when the finger hit the thumb—first the forefinger, next the middle, then the ring finger: "Ch"- "i"- "p." To conclude, the thumb would run across all three fingertips showing how the students were meant to connect all the sounds together to create the word, "Chip." In the lesson students would learn about vowels, glued sounds—like "ung" and "ing"—and how "ee" and "ea" may make the same sound but are used differently based on the consonant letters that precede or follow the sound.

I watched in delight as students tried hard to spell a new word, often getting tripped up by basic finger tapping. Their minds were sponges learning this new language. A language that, as an adult, I realized I had taken for granted. I tried to think back to the time when I was like them, unaware of English language fundamentals, and wondered what it felt like to be restricted by my capacity to properly articulate my feelings in written form. What it was like during the developmental stage of life when you are suddenly able to run faster and longer, write short morning reflections in a notebook, and are cognitively able to make connections and ask questions about the big world around you.

Watching my students begin to take hold of their world, starting with understanding the language that was needed to be a productive citizen, reminded me of my own developmental journey in the Darkness up to this point. It was as if for the last two years I'd lived in D.C. I had been tapping out new sounds trying to formulate words that described my new lived experience.

In relearning the rules of our language I was invigorated by how a word so small, made up of various sounds, would allow my students to understand their world differently. How words contain power in their own way. There was one word in particular that was having a similar effect on me.

Within the first few weeks of City Year orientation, each Corps member was given a spiral-bound handbook covering the pillars and values that would guide our year of service. As I browsed the pages I stumbled upon a core value—one word—I had never heard before: *Ubuntu*. This Zulu word was described in the handbook to mean, "I am a person through other people: my humanity is tied to yours." It ultimately conveys a message that stresses there is no "us" versus "them," but rather just "us."

Ubuntu conveys a message of mutual caring and responsibility and the concept that a person cannot be complete if others do not enjoy full humanity. The Senior Vice President and Dean of City Year at the time had written, "If one group within society is denied its humanity then no individual can fully realize his or her own humanity. The urgency to change this injustice becomes paramount." As if my heart had been hit by one of Cupid's arrows, my eyes became instant hearts, excited to finally have the language to illustrate the empowering interconnectedness of my experiences in Jamaica, Guatemala, Miriam's Kitchen, and what my City Year experience would soon become.

I reflected on this idea of "tied humanity." How in the Darkness—a place I felt broken—my heart was left armorless, vulnerable. And it was in these moments without armor that I was actually able to learn and connect the most willingly I'd ever been able to in my life.

There is something powerful about standing in the Darkness, lost. Something powerful about being stripped of old stubborn ways, that ultimately allows our hearts to open and become vulnerable seekers. Not because we are reading sticky notes posted on the mirror as daily reminders to "be vulnerable today" or "lean into discomfort," but because when we are in survival mode, our bodies are unwillingly stripped of comfort due to something out of our control, and we are left blindly searching, ultimately forced to rely on our basic senses to lead the way.

As a seeker desperate to find some light and comfort, my body found the purest form of healing in something that we all deserve in our life: belonging and human connectedness.

Learning new words, like Ubuntu, was just the beginning of the challenge that was putting my newly tapped words into full sentences and reframing previous knowledge. For a while I hoped I would further understand the meaning behind *why* Dad passed away so early. *Why* Mom lived with a chronic disease and was absent during a time in my life when I really needed an adult. *Why* I couldn't love Alex the way I wanted to. But perhaps it wasn't about "why me," but a larger question I needed to be asking—one that activated potential and empowerment: *What is my purpose? Who is the person I was created to be? How do these experiences inform my identity?*

While these questions remained unanswered, watching my students slowly learn the foundations of language gave me hope. They were gentle daily reminders of resilience and perseverance. Like sponges, they actively engaged with the world around them, both inside the classroom and outside on the playground. Perhaps, in my own journey, developmentally I was only a child recreating my foundation, re-seeing the world.

◇ ◇ ◇

After ten months and 1,700 required service hours, I made it to the end of my AmeriCorps year. Getting dressed for the graduation ceremony, I put my khakis on for the last time and applied my typical thirty-second make-up routine: a line of black-brown eyeliner where my eyelashes meet my eyelid and a quick upward brush of mascara.

Caught off guard for a second by my reflection, I stared into the mirror.

I saw Mom's natural beauty and Dad's ruddy skin tone, with slight puffiness under my eyes. Deep in my eyes, the part of my body I cherish most, I saw his joy for life and her fight—these central ingredients created in my genes that form the person I am. Refocusing my gaze, I stared at the part of myself framed in the mirror from my neckline up—at the person I was meant to be but had yet to fully know. The person that is a mix of shyness and confidence, of pensiveness and power. My inner knowing whispered songs of potential greatness, but my mind was still untrusting of what was to become.

As I reflected on my growth over the past few months, I thought back even further to the growth I'd made over the three years since Dad's death. The times when I felt broken and lost, only to find courage and hope in skydiving, Guatemala, Miriam's Kitchen, and my second grade class with City Year. These empowering experiences positively transformed my identity, and as a result, seemed to fundamentally change the way I viewed "Darkness."

In reflection, it seemed as though the most beautiful pieces of my life were a product of living in this space of unknown, a place I'd deeply feared. My protection, as an adolescent, was formed using perfectionism to create an airtight container free of failure, shame, unworthiness, and grief. But perhaps by fiercely avoiding these feelings, I was ultimately restricting my true potential and purpose. I'd imagined Darkness as an ominous, haunted, and lonely space experienced by those who were unfortunate to escape its wrath. However, the last three years seemed to suggest that the Darkness actually illuminated life's greatest treasures.

Just like dreaming, it seems that sometimes the wonders of the world show up to us more often in the Darkness, gentle gifts to help reassemble a new normal. The woman in Guatemala was my kindling, the internal material I needed to start a fire. The guests experiencing homelessness, whose hands held the trays I served food onto, were the first flickers of a flame. And my students were the bursts of light I needed to work my way out of the Darkness.

Looking back in the mirror I finally felt ready to take the step needed to claim my purpose. I felt deep within that my being existed for a reason. This newfound purpose existed as a result of my personal shattering.

Noticing my posture shift upright, my chin slightly raised, I no longer saw myself as a shadow in the Darkness, but as a created gift. As I considered the twenty-four year old I had become, for a brief moment, I saw my dad and my mom—the joy and the fight—the key pieces needed to create the foundation of the new me, the version I was created to be, staring me right in the face.

Part Three

P A L A C E

"The most beautiful people we have known are those who have known defeat, known suffering, known struggle, known loss, and have found their way out of those depths. These persons have an appreciation, a sensitivity, and an understanding of life that fills them with compassion, gentleness, and a deep loving concern. Beautiful people do not just happen."

—Elisabeth Kubler-Ross

Twenty-Two

Following my heart's desire to make an impact in marginalized communities and inspired by Ubuntu, I enrolled in a graduate program in community development that would begin the summer of 2016 in Nashville.

I'd come to the point in my journey where time had naturally healed deep wounds. The mountains of grief I'd overcome were clearly visible when I reflected on the past. I had battled the intense grief of losing Dad and also losing Mom as she continued to be absent—a soulless shell of the person she once was. Her health remained stagnant, but as I got older Mom's suffering seemed less related to disease and more related to the several intense pain medications she had been taking over the years. Observing this change in her, I often relied on Lumlum as a safe vessel to share my concerns, sadness, and confusion. Acknowledging to another person for the first time what I had hypothesized for a few years but never wanted to admit out loud, I was validated when Lumlum mentioned that part of Mom's dark shadows came from addiction.

It's a weird place to be a child and have a parent dealing with addiction. On the one hand, I knew I couldn't force her to get help for a problem she did not see, but I was also worried the day would never come where she would see it for herself and get the help she needed. As a daughter, this put a wedge in our relationship. She would often get frustrated when I acted like her parent, always saying to me, "Stop trying to be my mother. I already have one of those. I don't need two of you." But being her daughter, I felt continuously let down by her inability to meet the expectations I had set for her as my mother.

After so many years of patience, I caught myself feeling frustrated. I knew it wasn't her fault, but I was tired of waiting for her to acknowledge my personal growth. I was tired of feeling helpless against her disease and the medicines I knew she needed to take but would ultimately make her sluggish. I wanted more *for* her—that she could be free and happy—but I also wanted more *from* her—I wanted a mom that could help me navigate life's challenges, or at least listen to my boy problems.

Since saying good-bye the night in D.C. under the stars, Alex and I had continued talking, texting here and there when things came up that reminded us of one another. The foundation of our relationship remained largely unchanged: it was always complicated. I didn't have the emotional capacity to end things officially. Alex had become such a central crutch in my life, holding me up in times of deep grief and uncertainty. And yet, past emotions seemed to suggest I wasn't ready to be all in—the last time I had seen him in D.C. my heart was absent of the love I so wished I had.

In the three years we had known each other there was only one month where we tried to cut all ties, knowing our continued streams of texts inhibited us from moving on. That month of silence ended when a surprise box arrived at my door—new graduate school swag and a note of congratulations from Alex encased. This box reopened our complicated relationship, and as he had done in many other challenging seasons of my life, Alex helped ease my initial fears about making the move to Nashville.

When I first read about Vanderbilt's Education graduate program it felt like divine intervention—a place where I could put theory and research to the life-changing experiences I had in the Darkness. It was an appropriate next step in my journey to reassemble my identity—a clear next step forward.

After choosing a pursuit that aligned with my new feelings of purpose, my grief felt lighter and less in control of me, like I was regaining my ability to captain my own ship. I moved into a two-bedroom house in a tree-lined neighborhood in Nashville with a friend from college, made new friends quickly, and got a job as a teacher's assistant for an undergraduate professor—all providing me with reassurance and confidence that I was capable of navigating this next life chapter.

My feet felt like they were finally almost on the ground, something I was proud of. I intentionally worked hard to listen, to find the small moments of joy in the remaining pockets of uneasiness that accompanied first-time experiences, and to open my heart with the hope it would continue to heal. At this point, I knew I deserved happiness, and desired to feel rooted and secure—for something inside to just click. And yet, there was an inexplicable gap that kept my feet from fully digging in. A force that prevented me from feeling true authentic happiness. This undeniable force was fear.

Every time I wanted to let myself experience true happiness I was scared, fearful of being bulldozed by yet another phone call that would shake my world again. Like a marionette, my daily movements felt my own, but fear remained in control, manipulating my hands and feet with invisible strings so I was unable to fully live the life available to me, just out of my grasp.

Every time my phone vibrated my heart skipped a beat. Was my sister calling to tell me Mom was back in the hospital? Was my grandmother calling to tell me my sister had been in a car accident? Fear always painted pictures in my head of a loved one suddenly dying or being fatally injured. I was consumed by the idea that like a roller coaster, the longer I went up—the more days that passed where I was happy—the steeper the slope would be coming down. This fear that something was going to come crashing down any minute devoured me. I purchased a FitBit, which vibrated against my wrist every time I received a call or a text from my phone. This allowed me to view who was calling on the small black screen rather than having to disruptively search for my phone in my backpack during a lecture, or in the worst case, miss an important call or text completely.

Another life-altering phone call hadn't come. My roller-coaster theory hadn't proved true. While I was trying to live with an open heart, I was unwilling to be completely shattered again.

How would I conquer this paralyzing fear? I remembered the empowering love and faith I found in the Spirit when I was in Guatemala, and I sought a church with the hope it might rekindle my faith.

◇ ◇ ◇

I had not entered a church with the intent to open my heart and listen since my friend delivered her sermon. Though I attended various Easter and Christmas services in college, it took me almost four years until I was able to feel at ease sitting on a church pew. Instead, God and I were continuing to get to know each other where we first truly met: in nature. However, life was continuing to evolve. As a twenty-five year old still trying to answer the big question, "What am I supposed to do with my life?," I began dedicating weekly time for reflection by attending a Sunday morning church service.

The casual auditorium-like room made it easier for me to feel at ease. I chose a seat in the second-to-last row tucked in the middle so it wouldn't be too obvious I had come alone. Contemporary hymns, like the ones I sang in Guatemala two years prior, filled the space with authentic joy as souls of the congregation sang out. With each word I softly sang, I could feel my body release tension and my heart surrender its protective casing, my daily armor melting away. I welcomed the spirit enhanced by community, connection, and love.

Because I didn't know anyone, my fear of what others thought was not important. This Sunday exercise was for me and no one else. It became a sacred time for worship, but also a treasured time for my own self-development through listening and written reflection.

One Sunday, the pastor focused his attention on a central question I had frequently asked myself after losing Dad: *"Does God really care about me?"*

My experience in the Darkness—which I now understood to be a time of meaningful, vulnerable wandering—proved to me that God cared, but I was still searching for the deeper meaning behind the challenging events in my life, still struggling to understand my greater purpose.

The pastor's message was focused on one key point: how God loves and cares for the *real* you.

What does this real *me, the* real *version of myself look like? Will I know if I am living the most* real *version?*

After my dad died I was desperate to find any version that felt grounded, desperate to feel normal again. But was I actually seeking the *real* me? Perhaps I couldn't define her. What defined *real* anyway?

As if reading notes I'd scribbled during the sermon, the pastor elaborated on his simple yet complex statement by sharing a C.S. Lewis quote. Little did I know that Lewis' words would completely reshape my understanding of my lived experience and allow me to make meaning of the losses in my life:

"Imagine yourself as a living house, God comes in to rebuild that house. At first, perhaps, you can understand what He is doing. He is getting the drains right and stopping the leaks in the roof and so on; you knew that those jobs needed doing and so you are not surprised. But presently He starts knocking the house about in a way that hurts abominably and does not seem to make any sense. What on earth is He up to? The explanation is that He is building quite a different house from the one you thought of—throwing out a new wing here, putting in an extra floor there, running up the towers, making courtyards. You thought you were being made into a decent little cottage: but He is building a palace."

Using the words of C.S. Lewis, the pastor illuminated a cottage on luscious, green, open land. He explained that while we may enjoy living in this cottage, God is building us a different life than we envision, a life where we can be our most real selves.

My pen ran rampant in an attempt to write down all my mind was processing. It seemed C.S. Lewis was suggesting that, try as we might to build ourselves into a cottage—a decent place of serenity and safety—God has bigger plans and is building us into the palace God knows we deserve.

A palace isn't something we are equipped to build on our own because it requires a transformation of such magnitude for the original foundations of the cottage—your identity, the person you thought you were supposed to be—to be completely reconstructed into who you were *created* to be.

Suddenly, I no longer saw myself as a bulldozed cottage with shattered walls, windows, and doors. Instead, my pieced-together, reassembled identity was actually the beginnings of my Palace— the person I was created to be. One powerful image imbued my story with meaning I'd been searching for. Purpose.

This reframing consumed my thoughts. It was as if my entire world had been turned upside down. The next day on a morning run, glazed in sweat under warm summer sun, I chewed on this idea of *realness* in relation to the palace metaphor. Realness seemed to be what I experienced in the Darkness—a time where I was living vulnerably in the realm of grief and discomfort. I thought about my Cottage. How, for most of my life, I tried hard to avoid shame and discomfort by striving for perfection because I wanted so badly for my life to look just like everyone else's: *normal*.

My Cottage was initially constructed using the blueprints of the life I wished I had. A family of five all living together under one roof where I would wake up and smell delicious pancakes before school. A life where my mom packed my lunch box with a sticky note inside that said she was proud of me. A life where we went on family trips and ate family dinners around the table, chiming in about our days. A life where Mom didn't have a disease and we didn't have to worry about whether or not a given hospital trip would be the last.

I constructed this "normal" life by coloring inside the lines— following the rules, keeping to my space, not daring to ruffle any feathers. To remain not too loud, but not too quiet. To be everything to everyone without making it look hard. I followed my peers—from fashion to sports to romance. I wanted to belong. To be ordinary. To mask all the chaos at home in order to appear just like everyone else. I constructed and decorated my Cottage by allowing others to define who I thought I needed to be. And then I compared my life to that structure and, unknowingly, became trapped inside. In a literal and figurative way, I contorted myself to become what I imagined as the perfect Cottage.

Like an architect, I designed perfectionism, control, and self-reliance as the foundation of my walls. I didn't think twice about whether or not that was a life I wanted to live because in my eyes a life worth living was determined by outside approval. I sought approval like a drug. Trying harder and harder to achieve this model of perfection. But that's the thing. Did this Cottage resemble what I was created to be? It seemed C.S. Lewis was arguing otherwise.

My running pace quickened as the movement of my legs mirrored the movements of my thoughts running deep inside. *What defines "normal"? Is there really a standard form of living?* My younger self looked to external influences to create this standard for me: movies, TV shows, magazines—and my lived environment. My friends had two parents living under one roof growing up, moms that weren't sick, and later, dads that were alive. But it seemed my younger self was chasing a false sense of normalcy. Experience had proven this standard was a fallacy.

While my life may not have felt normal, I now realize so much goes on behind closed doors we often aren't privy to as outsiders. Everyone is dealing with their own challenges, sufferings, or insecurities, but, like I did, we often choose to keep these things hidden, ultimately perpetuating the manufactured idea that "normal" exists.

When Dad died my structure collapsed. My Cottage—the foundation of my identity—was bulldozed. The culturally-influenced decor and my well-armored door were smashed into tiny pieces, leaving me empty like a cleared plot of land. My soul felt dead, as though it had been buried beneath the soil trapped in Darkness. And yet, in this phase of suffering, I was unable to deny the transformative experiences I had. Skydiving and my trip to Guatemala were living proof that daring greatly—leaning in to vulnerability in the uncomfortable and unknown—can bring so much more joy, wisdom, and fulfillment than remaining in the space of shielded comfort. These moments served as the cornerstones for the new foundation that would become the beginnings of my Palace—its blueprint only unveiled with experience.

What if God constantly provides authentic, raw, beautiful opportunities, but we only see them if we courageously embrace discomfort instead of fearing it?

In awe of this epiphany, my running pace slowed to a walk. I needed a moment to breathe through my thoughts.

I'd recently read Dr. Brené Brown's book, *The Gifts of Imperfection*. Inspired by the book's thesis—that embracing your imperfections and working towards wholehearted living is founded on courage, compassion, and connection—a particular line in the book stuck with me, rumbling in my heart and mind: "To practice courage, compassion, and connection is to look at life and the people around us, and say, 'I am all in.'"

If this is true, I silently processed, my interest piqued in what was unraveling on my run, *and if raw, real, authentic experiences of courage have the ability to bring us closer to the most real versions of ourselves—our Palace—where, then, am I fearful? Where am I denying myself joy? And how can I be all in?*

Twenty-Three

"**C**razy that you would call. I was just thinking about you," I said, answering Alex's phone call a few hours after experiencing the epiphany on my run.

Having just finished thinking about where in my life I might be denying myself joy, it was hard not to think about Alex and our roller coaster of a past.

Was I denying something that was meant to be because I was scared? He seemed so sure of himself, so sure of us; why wasn't I?

For a while, I believed we weren't able to be on the same wavelength because I was an untethered soul. But there was something about my move to Nashville that allowed me to reevaluate—to gather momentum in the familiar environment of education and regain a sense of worthiness. With the C.S. Lewis quote fresh at the forefront of my brain, I felt rooted enough to further process this image of powerful transformation. *What did my Palace look like? Who and what form the foundational pieces that create the* real *me?*

I thought about people—those in my life who brought out the best in me and loved me unconditionally, even when I felt like a sobbing blob of emotions after Dad passed. There was no denying that one of those people was Alex, so what was holding me back from being all in?

Alex's phone call wasn't unusual in those months. Since moving to Nashville, we had talked almost every week to check in and share how things were going. After the pastor's message, I wondered if this phone call was a sign, a moment where I needed to build the courage to defy the "rules" of our so-called friendship and ask if he wanted to come and visit. I hoped that if there was any potential for us it would make itself known if we reconnected in person. My suggestion was met with an eager, "yes," and we made plans for him to visit two weeks later in early September of 2016.

When the weekend arrived, I picked Alex up from the airport in Nashville eager to show off my new life. A life I now felt more in control of. A life where I woke up to explore my new identity as a researcher and change agent for communities and youth. We visited a local restaurant for lunch and walked around my running loop, where I often talked to him on the phone. This time, it was nice talking to him in person. Everything felt easy, like the fall breeze just starting to cool down the warm summer temperatures. After dinner, we watched a TV show and I laughed so hard my stomach hurt. My relaxed happiness initially caught me by surprise. Everything felt easy, natural, comfortable—something I hadn't felt in a few years, my heart guarded against potential heartbreak.

At the end of the evening we cozied under the covers, closing our eyes for sleep. Lying on my left side, he on his right, my heart raced. Even though we were facing away from each other I worried that the thuds of my heartbeat were vibrating the mattress, exposing the unexpected explosion of feeling that rushed over me.

My heart felt lit from within, something I had come to appreciate as the gift God gave me for us to communicate with each other. Just as I had experienced an undeniable fiery warmth from within—in speaking my truth, holding the woman's hand, serving breakfast to the homeless, applying to graduate school—I was overwhelmed with love for Alex.

Initially embarrassed, I thought to myself, *There is no way after all these years of confusing mess that on the first night seeing him in months I can just turn to him and tell him, "I love you."* So, I didn't. Instead, feeling absolutely ridiculous, but unable to hold it in, I turned to lie on my other side, facing his bare back, and traced out each individual letter with my finger, his exposed skin like a blank page.

I. L.O.V.E. Y.O.U.

Still beating in this vulnerable moment, fear, doubt, and self-criticism crept into my open heart seconds after resting my hand on the mattress. I wondered if he could tell what I spelled out.

Without saying anything, he turned over to face me, looked me in the eyes and said, "I love you too."

This was the true beginning of our forever story. The story I wasn't sure I was ever going to be able to have after feeling such brokenness. I was afraid that I would never be able to love again after Dad died; the heartbreak of losing someone I loved was too deep. But as this moment, and the four years prior to it demonstrated, divine timing has a way of introducing (or reintroducing) us to the people who are meant to play a role in our lives. However, we are the only ones who can decide to cultivate the courage to follow the way, just as I followed the yellow scallop shells and arrows on the Camino.

If there was one thing I was sure of, it was that I was finally all in for Alex Arnold.

◇ ◇ ◇

After completing graduate school, I joined Alex in Charlotte, North Carolina, moving in the winter of 2017. It was another piece that effortlessly fit.

Not quite ready to be *all* in, I moved in with MK, who had moved to the city after graduating from Sewanee, and I got a job at a non-profit working to surround students with support to stay in school and achieve in life. Alex and I continued to date, excited to no longer have to do the long-distance relationship that we successfully navigated over a year and a half.

Five years after losing Dad, I finally felt grounded. Charlotte was a place I felt I could officially make my home.

A year later, I started dreaming about a ring on my finger and what it would feel like to one day call Alex my husband. We had been through so many ups and downs and he had seen me at my all-time worst. Everything felt right and my beaming heart solidified that.

Alex proposed on the beach in Florida, while we watched the sunset in late December of 2018. Knowing how important they are to me, Alex asked not just my mom, but also my sisters for their permission for my hand in marriage.

While everything about the evening was magical, once wedding planning began to settle in, remnants of fear inside made me feel concerned about the commitment of marriage. Everything was going so well, but, in my experience, marriage was not something that lasted. I struggled to feel confident in my ability to maintain a long-term commitment like this one.

Thinking about the lessons I learned in the Darkness—the lessons taught in the building of my Palace—I leaned into the idea that try as I might want to control the situation, I could not plan the future. It wasn't a promised thing that we would last forever—nothing was—but I had learned it was more important to lean into the feeling of joy than it was to deny it out of fear.

As I expressed these fears to Alex, a voice inside reminded me of *real* living. How real living meant courageously confronting fear when wanting to hold back, wrestling with the uncomfortable and scary. In doing so we become more beautiful in the process.

My heart was telling me Alex was the one, and it confirmed his unyielding love for me—now it was my turn to courageously trust that it didn't matter what others in my family had decided worked or didn't work for them. It was time to build my own life, my own family, my next life chapters. It was time to live out the words I lovingly spoke on the beach in response to his proposal. It was time for my whole heart and soul to daringly say "yes."

Twenty-Four

Planning a wedding was a daunting task. I prepared myself to accept it would most likely be done by Alex and me. If Dad were alive I am sure he would have concocted creative ambiance and party favors that would contribute to an unforgettable experience for guests—like the personalized CDs, posters with friends' faces cut-and-pasted on models posing on magazine covers, or other party favor props he made for friends' birthday bashes—ultimately making his absence sting that much more. If the prior few years served as a clear indicator of what was to come regarding the involvement of my mom, I didn't even try to get my hopes up that things might be different.

Prior to our engagement, Mom continued to be absent, her mental and physical health deteriorating. She went in and out of the hospital and slept even more throughout the day.

Travel itself was challenging for her, as evidenced by several times throughout my life when Mom had planned extravagant vacations she wanted to take us on only to never go. As teenagers, my sisters and I knew her disease would consistently deny these dreams. Her health was too unpredictable, making it challenging to plan ahead. When we went to Florida to spend Christmases with Lumlum, my sisters and I would often coordinate arrangements so one of us could fly with Mom and get her packed weeks in advance in order to make her feel more comfortable making the trip. Once we arrived, the amount of energy she'd spend traveling would set her back at least three days, making a month's stay necessary to really make any trip worth it, unless it was to Florida once a year.

I am not sure if she began to realize this pattern and wanted more for herself, or if something else stirred her mind awake to the reality that she lived in her own darkness for so many years, but in Florida, the week before I got engaged she—having known this would be the week Alex proposed—approached the beach lounge chairs Warren, Baird, and I were sprawled out on in sunbathing bliss and said she needed to have a family meeting.

"Why now?" I grumbled under my breath, a little frustrated that this family meeting had to be in such a public setting, surrounded by other families who were also enjoying their time in the sun. But whenever it came to Mom, my sisters and I tried hard to put our discomfort aside and act with patience, because no matter what crazy thing Mom did or didn't do, at the end of the day we loved her.

Pushing irritation aside, I sat up in the chair and put my sunglasses on, bracing myself for what I knew would be some sort of serious conversation, as evidenced by the memorable family meeting where we were told Mom and Dad were getting divorced. Mom took a seat on the corner of Warren's chair, her eyes staring hard in the open space deep in thought.

Shielded from the hot sun under the large white-and-yellow

striped beach umbrella, I watched as Mom's lips began to tremble. She looked at the three of us, and vulnerably proclaimed the words out loud for the first time, "I am a drug addict."

I was stunned in shock, but also incredibly relieved by this sudden proclamation. Her words instantly unleashed the floodgates of tears I'd been holding on to for the last few years.

These five words would be the keys to getting our mom back.

With the support of a therapist, Mom worked hard in the eleven months following this announcement to slowly minimize her dose of pain medication. With each drop in dose, her clear-headedness increased, like watching a thick fog lift on a crisp fall day, ultimately unveiling beautiful colors of the changing leaves.

Mom's energy levels improved over time and she began to be more present, remembering things from conversations we had about wedding planning. I was even able to return to Delaware and together we picked out and assembled the formal wedding invitations. This may seem a small task in the grand scheme of the numerous decisions necessary for planning a wedding, but this to-do that we did together will always be something I treasure. It was the first step to feeling like I actually had a mom—*my mom.*

While I was not privy to the really hard days when she felt nauseous and drained from the detox, the fight I deeply admired in her as a child was back in her voice. She was ready to step into the ring with a reassembled tenacious drive and give it her all. This time felt different.

Rather than talking on the phone one time a month like we had while I was in college, we were talking almost every two weeks. The wedding became a healthy project for both of us to work on together, and after a good but hard conversation, she still gave me the autonomy to make my own decisions, respecting the self-reliance I had built into my identity over time.

While I was excited about Mom's new transformation, I remained cautious in protecting my heart from potential disappointment, not fully trusting the uncharted territory of her sudden improved health.

As the months whittled down and our wedding day approached—November 9, 2019—friends and family asked me what I was most concerned about. Room blocks? Floral arrangements? Menu items? They were ready to jump in and support. Unfortunately, the one thing that stressed me out the most was something no one could fix: despite her progress, I remained fearful that my mom wouldn't make it. That something would happen and she wouldn't be able to get on a plane to fly to Charlotte for my wedding. That on the "biggest day of my life" I would actually be parentless.

My anxiety about her potential absence stemmed from deep within, from numerous occasions when she couldn't be there that stacked one on top of the other. While she had shown tremendous improvement and was transforming into a healthy version of herself I had never met before, when it came to Mom, I had gotten my hopes up too many times to let this time be different. Her presence in Charlotte for my wedding weekend would be the ultimate test.

◇ ◇ ◇

The day she was scheduled to fly to Charlotte had finally arrived—a Thursday, purposefully planned so if Mom missed her flight I would have time to do some emergency planning if needed. She texted me saying she was in the Philadelphia airport; her friend had dropped her off almost three hours early so that she could settle in at the gate with plenty of time. Ironically, with all the extra time, I was concerned that she might fall asleep and no one would wake her up. Here was yet another moment where I felt bound by being a daughter and not her controlling parental figure. My insides were tightly wound with fear, anxiety, and hope.

"Please let this time be different," I wished as I lightly blew a fallen eyelash off my fingertip, relinquishing my fears to God.

Before I left for the airport to pick her up Alex reminded me, as he often did, that everything was going to be alright in the end, even if things didn't go as planned. But I was so tired of not having things go as planned when it came to her. I was tired of having to be flexible and adjust my emotions and expectations to meet her situation. This was my wedding. I wanted to be selfish. I wanted my mom at my wedding, and I wanted her to make it on the day that we planned, at the time we planned. Just this once.

I pulled into short-term parking at the airport, followed the signs to baggage claim, and asked the information desk for a piece of paper and a pen. In big letters I scribbled "Mother of the Bride" (or M.O.B, as she liked to abbreviate it, like some sort of code name). I took my place waiting at the bottom of the escalator, hoping it would be the one she would use to come from the main terminal to baggage claim. I scanned the crowds, staring intensely at each person that came down the moving stairs, my heart beating faster and faster with each face that was not hers.

Did she make it? Was she able to get on the plane? Will my entire wedding weekend be ruined by this one fear? She was not able to make it to any of my sorority moms' weekends, nor my college graduation, and I was okay with that. I let it slide because I knew having her in my life at all meant more to me than having her attend events that marked special moments. But this moment was one I didn't want to compromise on. She was my mom, the mother of the bride. My M.O.B.

I continued standing, my white makeshift sign shaking slightly in my hands. A woman wearing slim black pants and a gray striped sweater stepped onto the escalator. Her fashionable outfit, accessorized with a blue scarf around her neck, blue glasses, and a blue purse that hung over her right arm, made me pause, and I complimented her trendy-chic travel outfit in my head. I glanced at the woman's face and lost my breath. This thin, beautiful woman riding down the escalator was my mom. Not only had she traveled by herself, she did so looking like the mom I dreamed about. She resembled the person I saw in pictures when she was younger, the person I imagined she was on the inside but her body and drugs had never let her become, her disease devouring her since my sisters and I were young.

Spotting me, she waved as the steps continued to descend. I waved back, trying to hold back happy tears as I watched in admiration from my spot at the bottom of the moving stairs.

Since we were together five months earlier, she had completely transformed. A mother of the bride I never allowed myself to imagine because I assumed it was probably impossible. The portable IV machine that once was kept in a Vera Bradley bag strapped across her chest was gone. It was just my mom in this cute little outfit, looking healthy and excited to celebrate her oldest daughter. It was a miracle I didn't fully understand, but I felt blessed.

We embraced in a super-sonic hug—a special kind of hug that got its name when Mom would hold us in her arms as kids really tight. It was a hug so powerful that I imagined love could transfer from body to body. Locked in a tight embrace, for the first time in what felt like my entire life I was hugging my mom without her disease and extra baggage. I was hugging the person I always wanted her to be, the person I knew she deserved to be.

I snapped a picture of her in the airport holding my little "Mother of the Bride" sign, wanting to always remember the moment just in case it was too good to be true. I also had to send it to my sisters as living proof of this new person who had physically just entered the building, but also re-entered my life. This weekend would be about many new beginnings—the official start to my journey with Alex as partners for life, and the rebirth of my relationship with my mom.

Twenty-Five

The moment I had been dreading since the day Dad passed away stared me in the face. Minutes before, Alex and I were thriving in our element, swing dancing to the upbeat rhythm of Whitney Houston's "I Want to Dance with Somebody" for our first dance. Afterwards, Alex and his mother captured the dance floor for the mother-son dance. As the song came to an end, I watched them walk off to the side, leaving the dance floor open for my moment. The moment I was robbed of six years prior. But, in those six years, life had taught me that sometimes the moments that don't go as planned are the most real.

"This song goes out to the bride's father," announced the band leader, who was followed by Lou Bega's smooth, deep voice playing from the speakers. *Ladies and gentleman, this is Mambo number 5.*

On beat, Warren, Baird, and I spun on our heels to face the crowd gathered around the dance floor as we started to count with our fingers following the song's lyrics in a choreographed dance.

"One, two, three, four, five/ Everybody in the car, so come on, let's ride."

And that's what this part of my life has been. A ride. A ride where more people than I could imagine have jumped in my car and have been there to support me.

Looking out from the dance floor, boogieing it down like we did when we were kids dancing in front of my dad in his small living room, the emptiness and envy I worried about feeling was non-existent. I saw my mom, Lumlum, Alex, my uncle, Beth, MK, Samantha, Karen, and so many others who have been pivotal characters in my life story in the audience.

No, it wasn't a slow-waltzing father-daughter dance. My head wasn't nuzzled into my dad's chest feeling the authentic joy of a long-awaited moment. Instead, I was filled with something perhaps even more powerful—the courage and strength to laugh, love, and let go. How could I feel empty when I was surrounded by my community? The people who stood by me when I didn't even recognize myself.

The journey to get here was not easy, and I know there will continue to be tribulations in my life. But had all of these things not happened, I would not be who I am today. I would not have gone to the middle of a dance floor only trusting I knew half of the moves by heart. I would've thought I was embarrassing myself and would most likely be worried about what people would say. The dance wasn't flawless and the three of us certainly were not completely on beat, but our imperfections are what made it perfect, made it lively and *real*.

In the spirit of Ubuntu—I am because you are—I am who I am today because of so many people who have become a part of my journey whether they know it or not. Reassembling myself allowed me to realize that dancing in the middle of a dance floor on my wedding day to Mambo No. 5 with the two people who have walked with me for almost every part of this journey was more unique than anything I imagined my "father-daughter" dance would be. While I wish Dad could have been there in person, he was with me in my heart and in my shoulder shimmies, channeling his easy-going social energy. The dance was evidence of how the unexpected, unplanned, moments in life can be just as joyful—just in a different way than originally envisioned.

What I have come to understand (and appreciate) is that life is made of constant reassemblings: we break, rebuild, break, and rebuild. Glennon Doyle writes in *Untamed*, "I am a human being, meant to be in perpetual becoming. If I am living bravely my entire life will become a million deaths and rebirths."

Made for perpetual becoming, with each reassembling of our pieces we became closer and closer to a truer, more beautiful, more *real* version of who we are made to be. We must be brave when facing fear, for limitations created by our mind can stop us from fulfilling our true purpose that lies beyond the boundaries of comfort.

I was not meant to be a perfect cottage. When Dad passed away, God demolished my pillars of perfection and control—leaving me with nothing—so I could further transform into the version of myself I was created to live—the version I was made for. It is a version that is still assembling, and will continue to reassemble, as my understanding of life and self continues to transform with greater introspection. But at least in this version I understand that living vulnerably is living freely, and it is the greatest kind of living. It is *real* living. Real living deserves a Palace. A place to grow, shine, wonder, and break free from structured pillars that once confined me like chains. It's where love, vulnerability, connection, community, and passion fuse together to create resilient openness. Where hard-pressed armor is no longer welcomed and instead, I practice grounded confidence in taking ownership over who I am: a person who has faults, who fails, but who also perseveres with positivity and is worthy. A person who has intense emotions, but those emotions make me beautiful because they remind me of what is real.

Just as C.S. Lewis said, as a living house, God comes in to rebuild the cottage. You may not understand what is going on at first, but God is building quite a different cottage from the one you thought of. God is building you a palace.

Believe in your palace, for you are meant to be extraordinary.

Epilogue

There is more beyond the conclusion I imagined for my mom years ago. Today, she is filling life chapters beyond her predicted "ending," beating the life timelines given to her by doctors years before, beating the disease and the drugs that dimmed her radiant light. I am incredibly proud of her and am overjoyed that we can celebrate and share this newness together. A relationship reborn. She apologizes for the pain she caused, her clear-headedness providing opportunity for greater reflection, but, as I remind her, I would not be who I am today without her story—both the good and not-so-good parts.

Getting to know each other again as the people we are today felt uncomfortable at first, foreign. Currently, we enjoy "walking and talking," using our wireless headphones every Sunday, a ritual I have come to love.

I feared after Dad died that Warren, Baird, and I were left parentless, adult orphans who thankfully had each other. And yet, five words—I am a drug addict—in my opinion, changed our entire storyline. Mom began to get herself the help she needed on her own accord. She realized it was time to live again, and she lives today to do just that. While she could write an entire memoir herself, her story—her truth—is hers to tell, but it stands as another example, for me, of the extraordinary that lies beyond the darkness.

Note to Reader

Dear Reader,

We don't often openly talk about suffering. When sharing this idea of a memoir I was confronted by people who would say, "Wow, that is really brave of you to share your story publicly like that with the world." So I want to first say thank you for opening your heart to mine. For taking time to read my truth as it stands today. For me, writing this memoir was not the least bit scary, but incredibly empowering. Sharing takes the writing part one step further, and while that part does take bravery, I think about how as humans we often stuff pain, suffering, shame, sadness—the hard stuff—deep down into the pockets of our insides, pretending like they don't exist.

As a society it has become a norm to politely ask, "How are you doing today?" to which most answer with an automatic, "Good," or if you want to take it one step further to complete the dance, "Good thanks, how are you?"

But what if instead of answering, "good," "fine," "great," we actually shared what we were feeling with people who are genuinely asking? I am not suggesting we air our dirty laundry to the grocery store clerk who asks in the checkout line, but I wonder what it would look like if we more regularly shared our true selves with a trusted network of people—friends, families, neighbors, co-workers. Perhaps doing the hard, challenging, scary, heart-breaking thing of confronting our suffering—the thing putting us in the darkness—can actually help us further transform into a more true version of ourselves.

For as I have come to deeply believe, and ultimately hope I conveyed in this book, it's in the grueling grip of the Darkness—stripped of comfort and armor—that we have access to the most real versions of ourselves.

Love always,

Tilden

Acknowledgements

What is written is my lived experience. It is an experience for which I have so many people to thank, as the majority of them are not mentioned by name in the text for sake of narrative flow or privacy. In addition, the process of writing this memoir itself has been a beloved journey. Both are journeys that wouldn't have been possible without the loving support of so many people who have greatly impacted my life. I am so grateful for my community of family and friends, and for all those who have encouraged me along the way. It is a community that extends far and wide, and for that, I am forever grateful.

A special thanks to:

Warren, my number one cheerleader from the very beginning of this process. War, thank you for being the encouraging seed that instilled bravery within my heart. Without your incredible support I would not have been able to continuously believe in myself. Thank you for being a constant reminder of what it looks like to stay true to yourself.

Baird, when I look at you I am reminded of strength. You are and will always be wise beyond your years. You inspire me to keep going even on the darkest days. Never forget your powerful light, it truly brightens an entire room.

Mom, thank you for teaching me all that you did and for allowing me to be my most true self in these pages. Your courage and fight inspire me daily as I continue to watch you grow into the extraordinary person you are meant to be. I will always be your angel.

Dad, your spirit lives within me. You are my angel, my protector, and my inspiration to live every day to the fullest. Thank you for so many incredible memories. Your legacy lives on.

Alex, I don't know where I would be without you. You are my forever, my partner in crime, and my best friend. Thank you for reminding me daily that "everything will be okay." You are, and will always be, my very best "yes."

Lumlum, thank you for holding me in your arms over and over again. You are the most incredible friend, confidant, caretaker, protector, and grandmother a girl could ask for. You have been there for me, Lummy, when other adults in my life were absent, and for that I am eternally grateful.

Hornor, you continuously pick up the pieces time and time again. Thank you for your incredible organization, transparency, and constant support. And to Freddy, Morgan, and Faith for also being incredible extended supports who are always willing to show up.

Beth, you are someone who helped teach me what it looks like to color outside of the lines. You will always be an important person in my life.

Mimi, thank you for all your love and support over the years.

My Sewanee Angels, you are forever friends. Thank you for wrapping me with love during a time when I wasn't sure I could put one foot in front of the other. You all continue to bring so much laughter and joy to my life.

SAS crew, thank you for being key players in the building of my foundation. Our friendship is one where even after weeks, months, or years of not seeing each other, we can jump right back to where we left off.

And special thanks to the following people who helped make this memoir even possible:

Kathy Izard, thank you for your endless hours of coaching and wisdom. You are my writer-role model and fairy godmother. This book would not be possible without your support. Thank you for believing in me and for creating a space where authors can write and learn more about self-publishing.

Elizabeth Dickens, for your brilliant edits. The moment I met you I had goosebumps, as if everything was meant to be. Thank you for taking a chance on me and believing in my story.

Frederica Morgan Davis, for pushing the manuscript to the next level. Your expertise and love for words is something I admire. Thank you for caring for my thoughts just as you have cared for me over the years.

Beta Readers: Mary Kate, Morgan, Lizzie, and *Josh*, thank you for your dedication to my words at an early stage. I am so appreciative of the time you took to provide meaningful feedback.

Dissect Designs, thank you for this beautiful cover! You brought my words to life in one image.

Katy-Whitten Davidson, for your creativity. Thank you for your time and beautiful talent.

Kendra, thank you for always being ready to assist with any crazy idea I might have.

And to YOU, the reader, thank you for choosing this book, and for taking the time to sit with my words. I appreciate you more than you know.

End Note

While my story does not include therapy, it is not because I don't believe in it. Professional counseling is important and I highly recommend that anyone, not just those struggling or grieving, seek professional counsel if they are able to do so.

Notes

Opening quote:

C. S. Lewis, *Mere Christianity* (New York: MacMillan Co., 1960), 160.

Author's note:

Marianne Williamson, *A Return to Love: Reflections on the Principals of "A Course in Miracles"* (New York: HarperCollins, 1996).

Part I: Cottage

Joseph Campbell, *Reflections on the Art of Living: A Joseph Campbell Companion* (New York: HarperCollins, 1991), 20.

Part II: Darkness

Wendell Berry. *Terrapin And Other Poems* (Berkely, CA: Counterpoint, 2014), 36.

Part III: Palace

Dr. Elisabeth Kubler-Ross, *Death: The Final Stages of Growth* (New York: Simon and Schuster, 2008) 96.

Brené Brown, *Gifts of Imperfection: Let Go of Who You Think You're Supposed to Be and Embrace Who You Are* (Center City, MN: Hazelden Publishing, 2010), 21.

Glennon Doyle, *Untamed* (New York: The Dial Press, 2020) 77.

Recommended Reading

Big Magic, by Elizabeth Gilbert.

Daring Greatly, and *Atlas of the Heart*, by Brené Brown

Untamed by Glennon Doyle

Other grief books/resources recommended by friends:

Untethered Soul: A Journey Beyond Yourself, by Michael Alan Singer

What We Lose: A Novel, by Zinzi Clemmons

When Things Fall Apart: Heart Advice for Difficult Times, by Pema Chodron

Can't We Talk About Something More Pleasant?: A Memoir, by Roz Chast

Here If You Need Me: A True Story, by Kate Braestrup

It's OK If You're Not OK: Meeting Grief and Loss in a Culture That Doesn't Understand, by Megan Devine

Option B: Facing Adversity, Building Resilience, and Finding Joy, by Sheryl Sandberg and Adam Grant

The Year of Magical Thinking, by Joan Didion

Tear Soup: A Recipe of Healing After Loss, by Chuck DeKlyen and Pat Schwiebert

Tiny Beautiful Things: Advice on Love and Life from Dear Sugar, by Cheryl Strayed

The Boy, the Mule, the Fox and the Horse, by Charlie Mackesy

Heaven is for Real, Lynn Vincent and Todd Burpo

The Dinner Party: The Dinner Party is a platform for grieving 20-, 30-, and early 40-somethings to find peer community and build lasting relationships. Since 2014, The Dinner Party has connected more than 13,000 grieving peers to one another, including 2,000 since the start of the pandemic. To learn more check out: thedinnerparty.org

To learn more about pancreatitis and other pancreatic ailments, visit:
   The National Pancreas Foundation: pancreasfoundation.org

To learn more about organizations mentioned in the book, visit:
   Potter's House (Guatemala): pottershouse.org.gt
   Miriam's Kitchen (Washington, D.C.): miriamskitchen.org
   City Year: cityyear.org

Other inspiring non-profit organizations I've had the privilege to be involved in:
   PENCIL (Nashville): pencilforschools.org
   Communities In Schools: communitiesinschools.org

Tilden Davis Arnold enjoys writing as a way to explore life's everyday joys and challenges. She graduated with a BA from Sewanee: The University of the South (YSR!) in 2014. Tilden furthered her education at Vanderbilt University, receiving her M.Ed a few years later. Professionally, she loves building positive relationships with and advocating for young people in various non-profit spaces of youth development. Tilden lives in Charlotte, NC, with her husband and her playful golden retriever, Finn. To learn more, visit tildendavisarnold.com.